FACULTY-STUDENT
SEXUAL
INVOLVEMENT

FACULTY-STUDENT SEXUAL INVOLVEMENT

Issues and Interventions

Virginia Lee Stamler
Gerald L. Stone

SAGE Publications
International Educational and Professional Publisher
Thousand Oaks London New Delhi

For information:

SAGE Publications, Inc.
2455 Teller Road
Thousand Oaks, California 91320
E-mail: order@sagepub.com

SAGE Publications Ltd.
6 Bonhill Street
London EC2A 4PU
United Kingdom

SAGE Publications India Pvt. Ltd.
M-32 Market
Greater Kailash I
New Delhi 110 048 India

Printed in the United States of America

Library of Congress Cataloging-in-Publication Data

Stamler, Virginia Lee.
    Faculty-student sexual involvement: issues and interventions/
by Virginia Lee Stamler, Gerald L. Stone.
        p.   cm.
    Includes bibliographical references and index.
    ISBN 0-8039-7304-7 (cloth: acid-free paper)
    ISBN 0-8039-7305-5 (pbk.: acid-free paper)
        1. Sexual harassment in universities and colleges.   2. Teacher-student
    relationships.   I. Stone, Gerald L., 1941–   II. Title.
    LC212.86 .S83   1999
    378.1'2—ddc21   98-25338

This book is printed on acid-free paper.

98   99   00   01   02   03   04   7   6   5   4   3   2   1

Acquiring Editor:	Jim Nageotte
Editorial Assistant:	Heidi Van Middlesworth
Production Editor:	Sherrise M. Purdum
Editorial Assistant:	Nevair Kabakian
Typesetter/Designer:	Lynn Miyata
Indexer:	Juniee Oneida
Print Buyers:	Esther Papegaay/Jill Ramey

Contents

■ CHAPTER FIVE
Issues and Interventions   **75**

Preface

We wrote this book for several reasons. Our intention was to develop a text that addressed the topic of sexual relationships between faculty and students in a way that could be used as a resource by the university community. By focusing on the major mission of the university, that is, creating the best possible learning environment, we can approach the topic from a common goal. The perspectives of professors, students, and the institution need to be understood for members of the community to empathically address the topic of sexual intimacy in the academy.

Our experience as students, faculty members, administrators, and therapists have provided some of the motivation for creating this text. As therapists, we have worked with distressed students who are experiencing the pain of broken relationships with faculty members through which they felt special and prized for a time. It would be easy to base this text solely on our frustration, with our imposed silence due to student confidentiality issues. But, our empathy is not limited to students. We also have been faculty members and administrators in public state universities with strong traditions of due process and faculty governance. Sexual involvement between students and professors cannot always be reduced to a cartoon depiction of the "good" students and the "bad and the ugly" faculty. It can be, and often is, more complex and controversial.

What is it about sexual involvement between faculty and students that makes these relationships so controversial? Why is it that discussion regarding faculty-student relationships is so heated and policy so difficult to establish and enforce? When arguments are reviewed, from the mundane to the arcane, we believe that the topic is salient because it is primarily about sex and rights. Sex always has played well whether it is in the media, mixed with politics and politicians, or in the academy. Freud was an astute observer and was very aware of the power of sexuality. Sex draws public interest.

A second contributor to the controversy is the human value of freedom. It is often heard in contemporaneous declarations of "rights" or entitlement to make one's own decisions. This theme is captured in various rights of faculty (faculty governance, tenure), students (right to make decisions about one's own life, right to an educational environment that is not hostile), women (right to oppose those who make rules about one's body), citizens (right to associate with whom I desire), and so on. When you combine the exciting topic of sex with the compelling rights perspective (I have a right to have sex with whomever I choose), you will have controversy.

A final factor that contributes to the controversy is an increase in awareness of sexual harassment and other abuses of power. As a culture, we have become much more sophisticated in our knowledge regarding the damage of sexual abuse and are more willing and able to discuss and address issues involved. This knowledge and increased willingness to address the issues involved in abuses of power have resulted in a more public and media discussion, which contributes to the controversy.

And because it is controversial, it is difficult to write about. To date, there has been little empirical research or policy development in the area of faculty-student sexual involvement (Stites, 1996). Too often, students, faculty, and administrators experience procedures and programs about consensual relationships as aversive. For many students, university procedures and programs are perceived to be more about protecting faculty and the university than supporting, validating, and advocating for students. Some faculty experience outreach programs focused on sexual harassment training as a "guilt trip," designed to punish male faculty. And many administrators simply want unpleasant things to go away. It appears reasonable to acknowledge these perceptions and avoid relying on sexual morality and gender politics as the major rationales for educating our learning communities. These rationales, although making useful contributions and used in this text, tend to deflect the discussion away from an educational context to one of "political correctness" and perpetrator or victim stereotypes. For example, in a gender analysis perspective, the perpetrator is seen as a male faculty member and the victim as a young female student (Dzeich & Weiner, 1990). The published data would support this scenario. But the gender analysis scenario may blind us to other forms of harassment (e.g., same-sex faculty-student harassment), as has happened in the domestic violence literature (e.g., Renzetti & Miley, 1996).

So, it is imperative that we be as clear as we can about our perspective. We are psychologists and write, more often than not, from a psychological perspective. But our writing is informed by faculty, student, and administrator points of view. We believe that education is the most appropriate context for discussing faculty-student sexual involvement. That is, the "coming and reasoning together" about good teaching surely provides a positive context for examining the complexities of human interactions. Good teaching is central to higher education. It provides the motivation for looking at practices (e.g., faculty-student sexual involvement) that might interfere with educating our students.

A difficult challenge for most writers in controversial areas is to address the question of balance. Does this text present a balanced perspective? This book is not a neutral, dispassionate, comprehensive research review. It is much more in the tradition of an advocacy resource text. That is, we hope that by providing an educational framework for examining relationships between faculty and students and delineating some of the key issues, this text will stimulate policy, practices, and research in this area. We believe that a greater understanding of the faculty and student perspectives is essential. A greater understanding of the impact of faculty-student relationships, including student developmental factors, would provide some important information. Another area in which additional information is needed involves the development and implementation of intervention programs for addressing sexual involvement between faculty and students.

Proposing one set of strategies to address faculty-student sexual involvement would deny the significant differences among communities and within universities, as well as between universities. Therefore, in this text we focused on delineating the key issues general enough to be useful to all members of the university community yet specific enough to provide information for individualized programmatic intervention and policy development. Thus, there are many things this text is not. It is not a research text, nor an intervention manual—although we hope our analysis is influenced by data and our recommendations have practical value. The book is not addressed to any one segment of the higher education community, but we have tried to interweave faculty, student, administrator, and student services perspectives. We do argue and take strong positions, but, again, we try to acknowledge the complexities and avoid easy answers. For us, the challenge is to balance an openness to our blind spots (e.g., gender analysis overshadowing same-sex relationships), at the same time avoiding deflection away from the current major problem: *some male faculty needs supersede some female students' educational goals while a majority of institutions of higher learning remain silent or too paralyzed to act.* In sum, we hope that the information in this text will stimulate college and university communities to further examine the issues and dynamics involved in sexual relationships between students and faculty and serve as a resource during this process. In order to accomplish this task, we have written the following chapters:

Chapter 1 provides an overview of the various perspectives of faculty-student sexual relationships held by members of the university community. This chapter considers the issue of professional boundaries and whether a relationship between a faculty member and a student can be consensual. The chapter also considers the scope of the relationship. That is, is a relationship between a faculty member and a student personal and private between these two individuals, or is this an issue for the larger university community? Finally, this chapter highlights some of the legal and ethical issues involved.

Chapter 2 examines a central component of the environmental context of the university community, namely, the faculty. The consensual relationship controversy is viewed within a faculty-based perspective. From a faculty point of view, the controversy arises because sexual harassment policy collides with the foundational values of the profession: academic freedom and faculty governance. Combining the traditional academic values of autonomy and collegiality with ingrained assumptions about social power and gender roles leads to a volatile context in which reasoned inquiry is replaced by acrimonious debate, denial, accusations, and litigation. Given these factors, faculty rights may seem more salient than faculty responsibility.

Chapter 3 explores the vulnerability of students. This chapter considers how societal factors influence students' perceptions of their professors and how these perceptions influence student-faculty interactions. Students often admire professors, owing to the knowledge they possess and their status within the society. Students also are taught to believe that faculty, as professionals, should be respected and trusted. This chapter describes the basis of this respect and trust and its effects on faculty-student interactions. Chapter 3 also addresses how developmental factors influence student-faculty interactions. Student development theorists tend to emphasize two primary developmental tasks faced by college and university students: the development of identity and the development of moral reasoning or values. Chapter 3 considers the impact of faculty-student relationships on these developmental tasks.

Chapter 4 considers faculty-student relationships in terms of the interaction of the dynamics of faculty power and student vulnerability within the educational context. The dynamics of faculty-student sexual involvement are considered in terms of faculty and student roles and gender. Because sexual involvement between faculty members and students involves establishing multiple roles with one another, this process creates relationships that are complex and ambiguous. This ambiguity, along with the power differential between the two individuals, places the student in a tenuous position. Because student-faculty relationships usually involve male faculty members and female students, the influence of gender needs to be considered. Gender-related power dynamics influence how men and women view themselves and how they are treated by others within the culture. Specifically, gender influences how faculty and students interact, including their expectations of one another and the academic environment.

Chapter 5 summarizes the key issues that we believe need to be addressed when developing intervention programs. We propose

4

interventions based on three fundamental tenets: (a) It is the university's responsibility to provide an appropriate educational environment, (b) intervention needs to be based on clear understanding of faculty-student dynamics, and (c) the goal of intervention is prevention of harm, rather than punishment. Interventions include education of the academic community, development of a consensual relationship policy, research related to faculty-student relationships, and reduction of isolation within and between university communities. We recommend concurrent interventions, including embedding broader educational interventions into ongoing institutional services that focus on good teaching and the importance of appropriate professional boundaries, rather than solely defining interventions in sexual harassment terms.

Acknowledgments

To my professors, students, clients, and colleagues who have helped me recognize the importance of understanding power, vulnerability, and professional responsibility. To Jim Nageotte and Sage Publications for their interest in this topic and their willingness to support this project. To Diana Pace for her significant contributions in the early stages of this manuscript. To Elizabeth Yarris, my friend and colleague, for her willingness to share her time, energy, and expertise. And to my son Colin and husband John for their unending support and encouragement.

Virginia Lee Stamler

To my students, clients, consultees, and colleagues for challenging me to learn more about the complexities of becoming a good teacher. And to the University of Iowa (including the University Counseling Service) for providing a nurturing environment for good teaching.

Gerald L. Stone

Introduction

I guess I started thinking about her because we kept running into each other. She's a new graduate student in the department, so we see each other a lot in the hallway, but we also have run into each other in several other places on campus and even downtown. When she sees me, she always stops to say hello and asks about my research or the book I'm working on. I never thought much about her until a few weeks ago. That night, I was coming home late after working all day, and she was just leaving a party at the apartment building next door. She was all dressed up and looked beautiful. She had been drinking and was being flirtatious. It was charming. She talked about how much she admired my work and how glad she was to run into me again. I could tell she liked me and I was flattered. We talked about common interests and I was surprised how much alike we are. I know the university discourages consensual relationships between faculty and students, and I agree with that for the most part. After all, faculty could use their power to exploit students. But, this is different. She's the one initiating a relationship, and I certainly don't plan to use my faculty position to harass her. We're almost the same age and she's a graduate student, not an undergraduate. In some ways, she seems more mature than I am. She's cer-

> tainly more confident. She suggested we might have dinner
> sometime and I said, "Sure, why not." Do you think that was
> a mistake?

I f this faculty member were asking you for advice, what would you
say? What factors would you need to consider? Are relationships
between faculty members and students different from other dating
relationships? Are relationships between faculty and graduate students
different from those between faculty and undergraduates? Does age
make a difference? Are these consensual relationships? Are these private relationships between two individuals or are these university concerns? Are there any legal or ethical issues involved?

Colleges and universities are among the most respected institutions in our society. As a culture, we place a high value on acquiring
and disseminating knowledge through research, teaching, and service
to the community. Through these functions, institutions of higher
learning have a great deal of influence determining not only what
information is important to acquire and pass on to other members of
the society but also how this process should be accomplished.

Thus, institutions of higher education possess significant power
and authority. Every member of our society is affected by university
personnel either directly through learning, research, or service or indirectly through instruction of our teachers, physicians, priests, phi-
losophers, writers, and so on. We feel comfortable granting power and
freedom to university personnel, owing to our respect for their knowledge and our confidence that they will act professionally and in our
best interest. Professors are given substantial freedom regarding what
they do and how they do it, owing to our respect for them as experts
in their respective fields. We give them titles to acknowledge their
status and achievements and to distinguish them from others. We trust
professors to make important decisions regarding one of our most valued assets: our brightest and most capable individuals.

Colleges and universities have a major impact on students. A summary of the available research suggests that this impact extends well
beyond intellectual domains to include a broad range of attitudes and
values that tend to persist throughout the student's life (Pascarella &
Terenzini, 1991). Much of this impact is due to the influence of faculty.

Interactions between students and faculty are an influential part of a student's university experience. Faculty have been shown to have a significant influence on the development of students' identity, their values, and their choice of careers (Pascarella & Terenzini, 1991).

Recently, one aspect of faculty-student interaction has become a major source of controversy on our campuses: Should faculty and students become romantically involved with one another? Opinions among college and university personnel vary widely, and decisions regarding policy and appropriate behavior have generated strong emotional reactions. Institutional responses to faculty-student sexual involvement vary, with some developing strict policies and guidelines about the practice and others ignoring these relationships. What is it about faculty-student sexual relationships that makes them so controversial? Why is it that discussion regarding faculty-student relationships is so heated and policy so difficult to establish and enforce? What factors need to be considered when addressing faculty-student relationships? How can we use this understanding to make more informed and appropriate decisions about student interactions, including faculty-student sexual involvement? If a professor finds himself or herself attracted to a student and feels that the student also is attracted, what should the professor do? A greater understanding of the dynamics of faculty-student relationships will help us make better decisions.

The purpose of this book is to examine the dynamics of faculty-student sexual involvement within the context of a learning environment. We will explore these relationship dynamics by considering the perspective of the faculty, the perspective of the student, and the interaction of these perspectives within the context of the university and the broader sociocultural environment. To provide a context for this exploration, this chapter will consider the nature of faculty-student sexual involvement and briefly consider some of the ethical and legal issues involved.

■ Nature of the Relationship

The way individuals and institutions view the nature of faculty-student sexual involvement influences how they would respond to the faculty member in the earlier example. The controversy about the nature of sexual relationships between students and faculty is reflected in four different (although sometimes overlapping) perspectives: (a) rights, (b) gender stratification, (c) sexual harassment or power, and (d) boundary violations. Each of these perspectives is held by some members of the university community and therefore needs to be addressed.

Rights Perspective

The rights perspective is based on the belief that students and faculty are adults and, therefore, have the right to choose to have relationships with whomever they want as long as these relationships are consensual. This perspective focuses on personal rights and includes the belief that the university should not legislate the private lives of its personnel. Individuals with a rights perspective believe that to forbid sexual relationships between faculty and students is to deny constitutional rights involving freedom of association and rights to privacy. Proponents argue that students and faculty enter into sexual relationships as equals and, therefore, sexual involvement between students and faculty should be treated in the same way as any other consenting adult sexual relationship. That is, they believe that the status of individuals, as faculty member and student, does not abridge basic and fundamental constitutional rights to privacy and association. An example of this perspective appeared in the *Los Angeles Times* (Sipchen, 1994), which reported on a group called CASE—Consenting Academics for Sexual Equity. Representatives of this group argued that to forbid faculty-student sexual involvement restricts an individual's right to date anyone he or she wants to date. The emphasis on *rights* in the midst of faculty-student relationship controversies is anchored in the foundational values of the past. First and foremost among faculty is the prized issue of academic freedom, followed by the empowering experiences of the civil rights movement, the women's movement, and student protests of the 1960s. These latter experiences, along with the reduction of the *in loco parentis* atmosphere, transformed our treatment of students from that of a protected group to that of individuals fully capable of making their own decisions.

Supporting the rights perspective, Keller (1988) concluded,

> The freedom to decline or resist intimate association is inextricably bound up with the freedom to form intimate association. Upholding both these freedoms in the university setting generates inherent conflict. Clearly, coerced intimate association is the most repugnant of all forms of compulsory association. However, the right to form adult consensual intimate relationships is a fundamental personal freedom. A strong and effective university policy against sexual harassment, together with the recognition of the right to privacy of faculty and students, will, within the parameters of constitutional guarantees, serve both the interests of the university and those of the individual. (p. 42)

Gender Stratification Perspective

The second perspective, gender stratification, examines faculty-student sexual relationships within the context of the larger sociocultural environment (see Hoffman, 1986). Advocates feel that restrictions placed on relationships between faculty and students promote a view of women as needing protection, incapable of taking care of themselves. These proponents believe that restrictions on these relationships reduce women's power and thereby perpetuate the inequality they are designed to address.

Hoffman (1986) made the following statement regarding amorous relationship policies:

> While they may be a well-intentioned effort to articulate community standards and to redress disadvantages previously experienced disproportionately by women students, they also constitute a basic abridgment of the right of students to be treated as adult members of the community. (p. 113)

Hoffman perceived policy that forbids faculty-student sexual interaction as reinforcing gender stratification within the institution and the larger society in which women have access to fewer resources and less power than men. Thus, viewing women as vulnerable to exploitation and needing to be protected perpetrates a system in which they will continue to be treated differently from men and, therefore, separated from resources and power. Hoffman argued,

> It is far more challenging and productive to endeavor to sort through the thorny issues of professional ethics, male domination, and sexuality . . . than to promulgate policies which reinforce status hierarchies and ignore or deny the rights of individuals to establish relationships when, with whom, and where they choose. (p. 14)

Sexual Harassment or Power Perspective

The third perspective considers sexual involvement between a faculty member and a student as a form of sexual harassment by the faculty member (see Dzeich & Weiner, 1990). Advocates of this perspective believe that sexual relationships between students and faculty never can be consensual, owing to the inherent power differences. This view reflects a broader conceptualization of sexual harassment similar to that adopted by the National Council for Research on Women (Siegel, 1991). Siegel quoted Fitzgerald and Ormerod, who stated,

> Originally thought to be limited to those relatively rare situations where women are compelled to trade sexual favors for professional survival, sexual harassment is now recognized more broadly as the inappropriate sexualization of an otherwise nonsexual relationship, an assertion by men of the primacy of a women's sexuality over her role as a worker or student. (p. 2)

An underlying tenet of the sexual harassment perspective is that "consensual" relationships in fact cannot be consensual, owing to the inherent power disparity between faculty and students. Students are in vulnerable positions with faculty, and what may be perceived as consensual in fact could be the result of direct or indirect pressure.

These power-differentiated relationships can lead to anticipated or unanticipated exploitation of the student.

Boundary Violation Perspective

The final perspective on faculty-student sexual involvement, and the one primarily used in this book, views faculty-student sexual involvement as a professional boundary violation. Peterson (1992) defined boundaries as "limits that allow for a safe connection based on the client's needs. When these limits are altered, what is allowed in the relationship becomes ambiguous. Such ambiguity is often experienced as an intrusion into the sphere of safety" (pp. 74-75).

Owing to the nature of the professional relationship between the student and the faculty member, students are in vulnerable, dependent roles compared with the role of the professor. The student trusts the professor to behave as a professional and to maintain appropriate professional boundaries. These boundaries are essential to maintain the professional relationship, and to violate or breach these boundaries damages the relationship, the surrounding relationships, and the educational environment. This perspective provides a way to view both men and women as vulnerable to boundary violations within the faculty-student relationship. It also provides a framework for considering how issues of multiple vulnerabilities can exist when the complexity of gender, class, ethnicity, sexual preference, disabilities, and age interact with the violation of professional boundaries. Specifically, an educational environment sets the boundaries for teacher-student relationships that creates a context of roles, structure, process, and atmosphere. That is, in an educational setting, there are teachers and students (roles) who gather at designated times and places (structure) for instructional activities (process) to occur in a safe and secure environment (atmosphere). Certain kinds of interactions, like teaching and learning, are set apart and distinguished from others. Sexual interactions with students are violations of appropriate educational boundaries within the instructional context.

The boundary violations perspective focuses on the necessity of professional boundaries to maintain the educational environment. The need for professional boundaries does not negate the importance of personal rights but emphasizes the need for professional relationships to achieve the function of the professional position, to provide the most effective learning situation. Individual rights are abridged only to the extent that is necessary to meet professional responsibilities. In personal life, boundaries are needed to establish and maintain identity, privacy, healthy relationships, and a comfortable interpersonal environment. Specific personal boundaries vary with culture. In professional relationships, personal boundaries need to be maintained, and professional boundaries also are necessary. Personal boundaries allow individuals to engage in personal relationships in a comfortable environment. Wearing clothing, closing doors and drapes, and not trespassing on others' property are examples of personal boundaries. Professional boundaries allow individuals to engage in professional relationships. When individuals take on a professional role, they also take on the responsibilities that go along with this role and, therefore, give up certain options. The gender-stratification perspective draws attention to the importance of addressing the underlying dynamics of a patriarchal society that promotes gender discrimination and the hierarchical structures of the culture, such as the university, which perpetuates this lack of power for women. Nevertheless, the gender-stratification perspective ignores the vulnerability of students within the educational context and denies the fact that professors and students are not equals. As Dzeich (1993) noted, "Clearly, we should try to inculcate courage and self-reliance, but we cannot demand that victims be stronger or more sophisticated than they are when the harassment occurs" (p. A48). The professional role involves power and, therefore, responsibility not to abuse that power. Establishing and maintaining appropriate boundaries is one of the primary responsibilities of the professional. Peterson (1992), referring to professional-client relationships, noted,

> Boundary violations are acts that breach the core intent of the professional-client association. They happen when professionals exploit the relationship to meet personal needs rather than client needs. Changing that fundamental principle undoes the covenant, altering the ethos of care that obliges professionals to place clients' concerns first. In fact, all of the

boundaries in a professional-client relationship exist in order
to protect this core understanding. (p. 75)

The focus on constitutional rights taken by the rights and the
gender-stratification perspectives is important when considering personal behavior, but it ignores the importance of professional responsibilities and the need for professional boundaries. White (1986) noted,
"sexuality is more than an issue of private behavior and personal
choices. Sexuality is always a dynamic in organizational families just
as it is always an issue in nuclear families" (p. 90). Sexual relationships
between faculty and students create dynamics that influence the educational environment and increase the possibility of damage to individuals, relationships, and the community.

Sexual harassment is one type of boundary violation. Thus, the
boundary violations perspective includes the sexual harassment perspective and also addresses areas not adequately covered by sexual
harassment policy, such as using the power and status of the professional position to meet personal needs that are not necessarily gender
or sex related. For example, a faculty member might ask a student to
care for his or her pets while he or she is out of town or ask a student
to give him or her a ride while his or her car is being repaired. Thus,
interactions between faculty and students can be exploitive, without
being sexually harassing. Universities need to consider the broader
context of professional boundary crossings and violations, including
sexual harassment, to understand the range of potential exploitation
of students.

■ What Is a Boundary Violation?

A faculty member's interactions with students can include a wide
range of behaviors. For example, a professor might single out a student
with a compliment, a criticism, or some other type of special attention.
This interaction could be public or private. It could be nonverbal, such
as a gesture or facial expression, spoken, written in reaction to an
assignment, or sent by e-mail or through a class listserv. Professors
might issue invitations to students or make a request, either singly or
as a group, either publicly or privately. For example, a professor might

invite students to be involved in a special research project, to attend a social gathering for a visiting speaker, to have lunch, or to share a room at a conference. These types of interactions might be confined to the content of the academic subject or they might become more personal in nature. For example, a professor might compliment a student's idea or his or her personal appearance. A faculty member might suggest that the student has great potential as a mathematician or as a good friend. A professor might request that a student participate in a research project or care for his or her children. A professor might pat a student on the shoulder to indicate a job well done or might offer a hug for support. Some faculty-student interactions are only personal, such as kissing, erotic touching, or sexual intercourse.

Which of these interactions would violate professional boundaries? Where the line is drawn is defined differently by different individuals and in different universities. Boundary violations range from inappropriate interactions to exploitive behavior. Three aspects of faculty-student interactions tend to be related to increased probability of professional boundary violations: (a) interactions that are more personal in nature, (b) interactions that put the student in a "special" role, and (c) interactions that place the faculty member's needs ahead of the student's needs. Interactions between students and faculty members should remain professional. Personal interactions create ambiguity and confusion regarding appropriate behavior and expectations. For example, personal comments, self-disclosure, or excessive touching or hugging by a faculty member can move the interaction from a professional to a personal one. Likewise, meeting with a student alone, outside the professional environment, can move the relationship from professional to the personal domain. Interactions that place students in a "special" role with the faculty member, such as a confidant or child care provider, increases the probability of ambiguity in the relationship and the potential for conflict of interest. Finally, interactions that move the focus of the relationship from meeting the needs of the student to meeting the needs of the faculty member usually are exploitive. As interactions between faculty members and students become more personal, deviate from faculty-student professional roles, or meet the needs of the professor, the possibility of boundary crossings or boundary violations increases. Gabbard (1989) suggested that non-sexual boundary violations may predict subsequent sexual boundary violations. It is the responsibility of the faculty member to establish and maintain an optimal educational environment. This requires appropriate relationship boundaries. Flirting with a student may seem innocuous to some faculty members, but this behavior can send a powerful message to a student: I am thinking about you in sexual ways. I am not thinking about you in your role as a student but as a potential sexual partner. How does this message affect the student? What effect does it have on other students? What effect does this have on the student-teacher relationship? If faculty members have questions about whether they are maintaining appropriate professional boundaries with a student, they should consult with a respected colleague.

■ Can Relationships Between Faculty and Students Be Consensual?

When considering how to advise the professor we quoted at the beginning of this chapter, we need to address the issue of consent. The faculty member in this example doesn't intend to abuse his power as a professional, but is this possible? Can a student choose freely? The student and faculty member both may view the relationship as one between two consenting adults, but relationships between professionals and those whom they serve contain an inherent power imbalance. A student cannot enter into a sexual relationship with a faculty member as an equal. Can a student ignore the status of the professor or the admiration she or he may have for her or his position? Is it possible to ignore the power the professor may have over her or his current education or future career? Peterson (1992) noted that noncoercive relationships require consent that is informed, mutual, and meaningful.

"Informed" means that all of the possible risks and consequences have been communicated and understood. "Mutual" means that the power in the relationship is equal. "Meaningful" means that the patient can say no without the possibility of harmful consequences to self, the treatment, or the relationship. (p. 124)

We believe that regardless of faculty and student intention, either or both of these individuals may not be aware of the risks and consequences of the relationship; therefore the relationship may not be "informed." The relationship is not "mutual," owing to the difference in power. Finally, the relationship may not be "meaningful" as defined by Peterson. Could the student be hurt if she or he later wanted to end the relationship? In sum, what may appear to be a consensual decision based on a decision between equals, is in fact not a relationship between equals and, therefore, not consensual.

Interestingly, a student's perception of whether or not a relationship is consensual may change over time. This suggests that experience or development may play a role in students' understanding of faculty-student sexual involvement. Glasser and Thorpe (1986) surveyed female graduate students in clinical and counseling psychology programs regarding their sexual intimacy with their professors. The authors investigated current and past evaluations of these experiences. Results indicated that 17% of the students had been sexually involved with their professors. Among recent doctoral recipients the percentage was 22%. Most of the respondents reported having seen no professional ethical problems at the time and having felt no coercion or exploitation. Nevertheless, judgments regarding feelings of coercion, ethical problems, and hindrance to the working relationship changed substantially over time. Although 28% reported that they experienced some degree of coercion at the time of contact, 51% later saw some degree of coercion. In addition, although 36% believed that the relationship was an ethical problem at the time, 55% later concluded it was an ethical problem. Thus, students may or may not feel some degree of coercion while involved in the relationship, but their perspective may change over time.

■ The Scope of the Relationship

Some individuals and institutions view faculty-student sexual involvement as a relationship between two self-contained individuals, whereas others feel that the relationship needs to be considered within a broader context of the university community. Sometimes, students who are aware of a relationship between a faculty member and another student feel they are not being treated fairly. They feel the student involved with the professor is being given special privileges from which they are excluded. To determine how the relationship should be addressed, it is necessary to establish whether it is solely a private matter between two individuals or involves institutional concerns. That is, if the relationship is personal and private, as suggested by the rights perspective, then any problems are between the two individuals involved. Nonetheless, if the relationship is viewed as a part of the academic community, then any problems become issues for the university. Interestingly, there are gender differences in faculty and student perceptions of the scope of the relationship (Paludi, 1990). Men tend to believe that faculty-student relationships are personal and between the individuals involved. Conversely, women tend to believe that faculty-student relationships are an institutional issue. The perspective of this book is that sexual involvement between faculty and students affects not only the two individuals involved but also the rest of the academic community as well as the larger society and, therefore, needs to be addressed within the larger context.

■ Ethical and Legal Issues

University communities need to consider whether there is something about the context of the university that makes relationships between faculty and students ethically or legally different from other dating relationships. By ethical, we mean what is appropriate, given the professional nature of the relationship. By legal, we mean what has been established by law.

Ethical Issues

Most professions within the United States have ethical codes that are the standards of conduct that members of the profession are expected to observe. Training in ethical decision making and knowledge of appropriate professional guidelines is often a part of the educational and licensing requirements for professionals. Typically, training in knowledge of appropriate professional behavior and ethical decision making is not a requirement (although an expectation) for becoming a faculty member. This is unfortunate, considering the impact of faculty-student interactions and the potential for exploitation. Like other professionals, faculty need information regarding ethical decision making and appropriate professional behavior.

The American Association of University Professors (AAUP) has developed a "Policy on Professional Ethics" for teachers in higher education (see Weeks, 1995). Although this policy does not specifically address sexual relationships between faculty and students, there are several principles within the policy with implications for these relationships if they are examined within the context of educational practice. The first principle of educational practice (with ethical statements in parentheses) is abstinence ("adhere to the proper roles as intellectual guides"). Accordingly, teachers in their interactions with students should refrain from personal need satisfaction that is beyond the professional satisfaction derived from being part of the educational process. A second principle of educational practice is interpersonal neutrality ("avoid any exploitation, harassment, or discriminatory treatment of students"). Teachers are discouraged from involving themselves in students' personal affairs that are outside the educational agenda. A third principle relates to autonomy and independence ("respect for students as individuals").

The AAUP *Statement of Professional Ethics* recognizes the power of the faculty member and the potential for faculty exploitation of students. Nonetheless, because the statement does not specifically address sexual relationships between faculty and students, faculty members and institutions do not have clear professional guidelines.

Other professions have developed very clear guidelines. The American Psychological Association's (APA) "Ethical Principles of Psychologists and Code of Conduct" (1992) is very specific regarding relationships between psychologists and those over whom they have power. Principle 4.05 states, "Psychologists do not engage in sexual intimacies with current patients or clients" (p. 1605).

The APA ethical principles and code of conduct goes further to consider the relationships between former clients and patients and their therapist. Principle 4.07 states,

(a) Psychologists do not engage in sexual intimacies with a former therapy patient or client for at least two years after cessation or termination of professional services.

(b) Because sexual intimacies with a former therapy patient or client are so frequently harmful to the patient or client, and because such intimacies undermine public confidence in the psychology profession and thereby deter the public's use of needed services, psychologists do not engage in sexual intimacies with former therapy patients or clients even after a two-year interval except in the most unusual circumstances. The psychologist who engages in such activities after the two years following cessation or termination of treatment bears the burden of demonstrating that there has been no exploitation. (p. 1605)

The APA ethical principles and code of conduct specifically address relationships between professors and their students. Principle 1.19 states,

(a) Psychologists do not exploit persons over whom they have supervisory, evaluative, or other authority, such as students, supervisees, employees, research participants, and clients or patients.

(b) Psychologists do not engage in sexual relationships with students or supervisees in training over whom the psychologist has evaluative or direct authority, because such relationships are so likely to impair judgment or be exploitative. (p. 1602)

The medical profession likewise recognizes the vulnerability of those they serve. The American Medical Association's *Code of Medical Ethics* (1996-97) states,

Sexual contact that occurs concurrent with the physician-patient relationship constitutes sexual misconduct. Sexual or romantic interactions between physicians and patients detract from the goals of the physician-patient relationship, may exploit the vulnerability of the patient, may obscure the physician's objective judgment concerning the patient's health care, and ultimately may be detrimental to the patient's well-being.

If a physician has reason to believe that non-sexual contact with a patient may be perceived as or may lead to sexual contact, then he or she should avoid the non-sexual contact. At a minimum, a physician's ethical duties include terminating the physician-patient relationship before initiating a dating, romantic, or sexual relationship with a patient.

Sexual or romantic relationships between a physician and a former patient may be unduly influenced by the previous physician-patient relationship. Sexual or romantic relationships with former patients are unethical if the physician uses or exploits trust, knowledge, emotions, or influence derived from the previous professional relationship. (p. 130)

The legal profession also has addressed relationships between lawyers and their clients. The American Bar Association's *Annotated Model Rules of Professional Conduct* (1996) notes,

The ABA Ethics Committee has issued an opinion that addresses the issues of lawyer's sexual relations with clients and concludes that lawyers would be well advised to refrain from such relationships. . . . The opinion states that a sexual relationship between lawyer and client may involve unfair exploitation of the lawyer's fiduciary position and/or significantly impair a lawyer's ability to represent the client competently, and thus may violate both the Model Rules of Professional Conduct and Model Code of Professional Responsibility. (p. 563)

The ABA's *Annotated Model Rules of Professional Conduct* also notes that the legal ethics committees of some state bar associations (e.g., Oregon) prohibit lawyers and clients from initiating sexual relations during formal representation. Joanne Pitulla (1992), Assistant

Ethics Counsel for the ABA's Center for Professional Responsibility, noted,

> Although deep pockets of resistance still linger, debate is moving from whether sexual relations between lawyers and clients ought to be regulated to how regulation should be done. Rather than distinguishing consensual relations from harassment, the emphasis is on a *per se* prohibition. There is a growing recognition that even under the best circumstances, these relationships can be inherently coercive. (p. 76)

The ethical statements of the American Psychological Association, the American Medical Association, and the American Bar Association recognize the potential damage of professional-client sexual involvement and the need for appropriate professional boundaries. To ensure safety and the freedom to learn for students in a deliberately unbalanced teacher-student relationship, the profession or the institution needs to establish professional boundary principles. In following these principles as an educator, sex with students represents a boundary violation. In essence, the establishment of a sexual relationship by a teacher with a student creates a dual relationship. Dual relationships include situations in which a teacher functions in a professional role (educator) concurrently with another "special" role (lover) that adversely affects the dynamics of the professional role. These relationships are damaging to the individuals involved, the professional relationship, and the university community.

Legal Issues

A detailed discussion of the legal aspects of faculty-student relationships is beyond the scope of this text. Nevertheless, we would like to review some of the more important legal decisions that relate to the issue of faculty-student sexual involvement. More than 30 years ago, the Civil Rights Act was passed. Title VII of the Civil Rights Act of 1964 prohibited employers from discriminating against individuals on the basis of sex. The adoption of Title IX of the 1972 Federal Education Act applied the principles and guidelines of Title VII to education

(Wishnietsky & Felder, 1994). This prohibited universities from discriminating against women on the basis of sex. In 1976, Yale University was sued by several female students, which set a precedent for hearing sexual harassment grievances under Title IX of the 1972 Educational Amendments (*Alexander v. Yale*, 1980, as reported in Wishnietsky & Felder, 1994). The students claimed that the university was responsible for preventing and dealing with sexual harassment within the institution.

In 1984, three administrators at Louisiana State University were sued by a female graduate student who was involved with a female freshman student (*Naragon v. Wharton*, 1984). The graduate student sued when she was reappointed to her position as a graduate assistant but without teaching responsibilities. The graduate student claimed that the university was discriminating against her on the basis of the homosexual relationship. The university denied this claim and contended that it considered any intimate relationship between teachers and students a breach of professional ethics. The district court ruled in favor of the university based on the view that intimate relationships between students and teachers are unprofessional and could be detrimental to students and the university (Hustoles, 1990). That same year, in *Korf v. Ball State University* (1984), a tenured professor was dismissed for sexual harassment, including involvement in a consensual relationship. The university cited the AAUP *Statement of Professional Ethics* to support the dismissal and disregarded the consent defense owing to the teacher-student relationship (Hustoles, 1990). The university noted the section of the AAUP statement that states, "As a teacher, the professor encourages the free pursuit of learning in his students. . . . He avoids any exploitation of students for his private advantage" (Hustoles, 1990, p. 3). The court accepted the university's defense of its actions and ruled in favor of the university.

On February 26, 1992, The U.S. Supreme Court unanimously ruled in *Franklin v. Gwinnett County Public Schools* that students who had been sexually harassed could collect monetary damages under Title IX of the 1972 Federal Education Act (Wishnietsky & Felder, 1994). Wagner (1993) suggested that it is extremely important for university and college faculty, administrators, and trustees to be aware of the potential liability they face regarding faculty-student sexual involvement. Wagner (1993) noted that even though administrators and trustees may be unaware of what is happening in a student-faculty relationship, they may be liable for any resulting damages to a student under the anti-sex-bias provisions of Title IX of the Educational Amendments of 1972 (although this assertion is in current litigation). Wagner noted that although students initially may view their relationships with professors as consensual, as they gain a more adult perspective they may reconsider the relationship and view it as sexual harassment. Glasser and Thorpe's (1986) study supports this possibility. Hustoles (1990) stated,

> It is your author's consensus that professional ethic concerns centered on the naturally exploitive potential of professor-student relationships, as well as policy reasons relating to good management principles in the employment area, serve as a sound basis for regulating such conduct. (p. 5)

Thus, both legal and ethical implications need to be addressed when considering student-faculty interactions. Sexual involvement between faculty and students is a violation of appropriate professional boundaries that interferes with the teaching and learning mission of the university. Therefore, faculty-student relationships, including sexual relationships, are an institutional concern. Because sexual involvement between faculty and students is a university concern and because the profession of faculty members does not have a specific ethical code addressing these relationships, the university needs to develop a clear institutional policy.

■ Summary

We emphasized the importance of examining dual roles and gender roles when considering the dynamics of faculty-student involvement. That is, the university is embedded within the context of different "cultures." Interactions between individuals within the university environment are influenced by, and in turn influence, the broader sociocultural context. For example, gender shapes the sociocultural context in which individuals live. Gender affects the interactions individuals have with one another and the opportunities they perceive are available to them. Gender-related factors influence interactions through predispositions, expectations, attitudes, and behaviors (Deaux & Major, 1987).

We would strongly advise the faculty member in the example at the beginning of this chapter to reconsider the dinner invitation from this student. We believe that the educational context of the university makes relationships between faculty and students different from other relationships. These differences are due to the nature of the faculty-student relationship and the specific vulnerabilities of students in the university community. Universities and their faculties have professional and ethical responsibilities to acknowledge and address these differences to provide an educational environment that is conducive to learning for all members of the society.

CHAPTER TWO

The Faculty Context

What do the following faculty statements have in common?

Administrators do not belong in the bedrooms of their faculty.

As a faculty member, I have a right to engage in personal relationships without interference.

Consensual relationships that do not affect the academic workplace are none of your (i.e., administrators) business.

The university cannot legislate faculty morality, no matter how loud radical feminists and the priests of political correctness scream.

Faculty accused of sexual misconduct by students are not treated fairly.

First, these statements describe issues of concern for many faculty members, as colleges and universities address faculty-student sexual involvement within the context of academic sexual harassment. Second, efforts to address consensual-relationship issues have been relatively ineffective and have created faculty resistance, because such efforts have not adequately considered the dynamic conditions that influence the campus environment (see Kuh, 1993). Third, consensual-relationship issues represent a flash point for the "culture and gender wars" in society. Fourth, these issues involve cultural phenomena, in that the behavior and attitudes of faculty in addressing consensual relationships are shaped by the culture of the academic profession and the larger social, political, economic, and historical forces that influence higher education and structure our lives. Thus, to develop a context of understanding faculty-student sexual involvement, we will examine faculty culture and larger sociocultural conditions.

As with most things related to academia and faculty, all-or-nothing definitions about faculty matters are bound to fail. Faculties are said to differ by type of institution (research university vs. community college), discipline (social science vs. natural science), appointment conditions (adjunct vs. tenured faculty), and gender, to name but a few (Austin, 1990; Boyer, 1987; Chamberlain, 1988). Given the lack of a well-defined faculty culture, a convenient way of thinking about such "fuzzy" categories is in terms of a prototype (see Rosch, 1973, 1978). A prototype may be thought of as the central tendency (typical) of feature values across all valid members of a category. With regard to faculty culture, the question concerns the features (general factors) that make up the prototype "faculty culture." The general factors that make up the faculty culture are taken from prior scholarly work in higher education and social science. We propose two clusters of features. One cluster, derived primarily from research and writings in higher education, has to do with the primary faculty values (Values Perspective). The second cluster, based primarily on research and the literature on academic sexual harassment, is concerned with gender, power, and other sociocultural phenomena (Cultural Perspective). Each feature cluster consists of values, beliefs, or both thought to be related to faculty concerns and, in some cases, resistance to consensual-relationship policies.

■ Values Perspective

Although debate continues about whether a common faculty culture exists, a number of core values have been identified (Austin, 1990). One of the key values of the academic profession concerns the purpose of higher education. That is, the pursuit, dissemination, and maintenance of knowledge are primary goals. Another central value espoused by the academic community is a commitment to improving society. These key values underlie the traditional academic responsibilities of teaching (dissemination of knowledge), research (discovery of knowledge), and service.

More germane to our topic are two foundational values of academia that have been developed, debated, struggled over, and intensely prized by faculty through conflict that continues to this day. The first contested and prized value is professional autonomy, including the importance of academic freedom. The other value is collegiality, expressed through faculty governance and peer review. These two values provide a framework for understanding some of the difficulties for faculty in addressing consensual-relationship issues. Before we undertake that particular discussion, a little more background about these more relevant values is needed.

The inspiration for academic freedom, and its expansion from a single freedom to freedoms, evolved from the unique American experience and was reinforced by the German university tradition (Rudolph, 1962). From an inspirational point of view, conflicts between academia and the larger community always have occurred, including early conflicts about the classical curriculum and sectarian interests and the new science, conflicts with the business community and unpopular causes, the controversies of the early 1950s about loyalty oaths, and the more modern-day issues of hate speech, sexual materials in the classroom, multicultural curriculum requirements, and so on. Emerging from the early conflicts, reinforced by the principles of scholarship in German universities, and implemented in later controversies, came the respect and importance of academic freedom to the life of the mind. To the value and principle of academic freedom in the early 20th century were added the structures of academic tenure and professional societies (e.g., American Association of University Professors) to protect faculty autonomy and academic freedom.

Originally, academic freedom (*Lehrfreiheit*) in Germany applied only to the professor and his (and later her) scholarly work within the university. In this narrow context, academic freedom came to mean the creation of a climate in which a scholarly point of view was dominant, encouraging tolerance for differing views and preference for experiment and inquiry over tradition or inherited wisdom. Nevertheless, the professor, as well as any other servant of the state, enjoyed no such freedom or related professorial privileges outside the academic walls. How different in America, where all Americans enjoyed the traditional rights of freedom. As a consequence, a modern and widespread assumption among faculty in American universities is that academic freedom is not one right but represents a charter of liberties entitling the professor to full autonomy, choosing what he or she shall do and when and having a dominant voice in all university matters.

This latter entitlement, collegiality, is espoused as the belief that the university is a community of scholars working together to govern the institution. Collegiality provides a framework for academic and institutional decision making and faculty interactions through which academic freedom is tempered by support of one's colleagues. As was the case with academic freedom, early academic histories report many battles between faculties, the president, and/or trustees about who would determine educational matters—curriculum, course content, selection of students, choosing faculty colleagues, and evaluating faculty for promotion and tenure. Today, faculty control over educational matters is pervasive yet not absolute. Most educational matters, including budgets and personnel, are subject to "higher" review, and ultimate control remains where it has always been—administration by governing boards and the legislatures. But many faculty see themselves (and students) as *the university*.

Combining the values of autonomy and collegiality with the role of faculty in higher education helps us to understand the special context of being a faculty member (Rosovsky, 1990). As tenured faculty, we often think about and practice our profession as a calling, considering ourselves not employees but a group of owners of the university or, in less grandiose terms, the major capital stock that needs continual investment for the building and renewing of intellectual capital. In such a special role and without much exaggeration, tenured professors do not have bosses as do employees: a boss who tells you what to do and requires you to do it. Today some professors claim they have too many bosses, from intrusive legislators and academic administrators to various pundits of morality and political correctness. But the general feeling is that a professor is not just another employee. Such a sentiment was given voice by a professor involved in the California loyalty oath controversy. Dr. Kantororwicz (as reported in Rosovsky, 1990), a former Professor of Medieval History at the University of California at Berkeley, wrote,

> Why is it so absurd to visualize the Supreme Court Justices picketing their court, bishops picketing their churches and professors picketing their universities? The answer is very simple: because the judges *are* the court, the ministers together with the faithful *are* the church, and the professors together with the students *are* the university . . . they are those institutions themselves, and therefore have prerogative rights to and within their institution which users, sextons and beadles, and janitors do not have. (pp. 164-165)

This quote underscores an aspect of the context of faculty response to consensual relationship policy, namely the "rights" perspective.

Rights

The regulation of consensual relationships by colleges and universities does not enjoy widespread consensus among faculty. From the rights perspective, regulation efforts may be well intentioned, but they constitute a basic abridgment of the rights of faculty to freely enter into intimate relationships with students. Certain faculty groups (e.g., Consenting Academics for Sexual Equity—CASE; see Sipchen, 1994) and constitutional champions (e.g., American Civil Liberties Union) assert that any attempt to regulate consensual relationships is not the business of colleges or universities. In fact, these attempts arguably violate constitutional rights or guarantees of freedom of association ("dating") or privacy ("right to engage in a highly personal relationship free from governmental intrusion") and might even raise academic freedom issues (Keller, 1988). Policies upholding the student's freedom to resist intimate associations in the academy are inextricably connected with faculty freedoms, including the freedom to form intimate associations. Moreover, administrative edicts about amorous relationships that come handed down without sufficient faculty input are bound up with the sense of loss of collegiality, peer review, and faculty control of the educational environment. It also could be stated that such administrative amorous-relationship statements constitute a basic abridgment of the right of students, especially women students, and women faculty to be treated as adult members of the community. Whereas policy can be liberating for many, too often these policies are experienced as forms of bureaucratic paternalism by many faculty, socialized as a special group with a charter of freedoms, and by many feminists and female students and faculty who "wish to choose whether, when, where, and with whom to have sexual relationships, as one important part of exercising control over their lives" (Mackinnon, 1979, p. 25). These latter groups, including many racial and ethnic minorities, are especially sensitive to paternalistic encroachments, given the history of disenfranchisement of students, minorities, and women in higher education. In response to these previous disadvantages, the student's and women's movements transformed the nature of higher education with the belief that treating students as adults and women faculty as full participants in the creation of institutional policy leads to enhanced accountability for the educational experience.

Responsibilities

In addition to the rights of faculty, faculty also have obligations. Historically, these obligations were construed broadly, from including character development and religious training in the colonial colleges to the *in loco parentis* point of view of the early 20th century. Faculty responsibilities included meeting all needs of students away from home, not only educational ones but those associated with a collegiate way of living (dependent on dormitories; committed to dining facilities; and permeated by a paternalistic attitude of caring for the morals, health, and safety of the student; Rudolph, 1962). In the modern era, faculty assert, "I am only here to teach my courses. . . . I have no other responsibilities." Thus, today's formal duties for faculty are minimal, anywhere from 6 to 12 hours per week in the classroom during the academic year (8 months). Of course, boards of trustees and state legislatures are pushing for more class-time instruction. And professors often work long hours on classroom responsibilities and on their scholarship. But the broad faculty obligations of an earlier time either have been delegated to a variety of auxiliary and student support services or canceled (e.g., *in loco parentis*).

What are the responsibilities of the faculty to preserve the academic integrity of the educational experience? Although there has been general acknowledgment in the literature about the classic triad of faculty responsibilities—teaching, research, and service—more has been written about faculty rights of freedom, autonomy, and self-governance. The American Association of University Professors (AAUP) traditionally has seen its role as defending the rights of faculty. Recently the AAUP's *Statement of Professional Ethics* has been used to address the questions of faculty responsibility (Connolly & Marshall, 1989) germane to consensual relationships. The statement provides (as cited in Weeks, 1995),

> As teachers, professors encourage the free pursuit of learning in their students. They hold before them the best scholarly and ethical standards of their discipline. Professors demonstrate respect for students as individuals and adhere to their proper roles as intellectual guides and counselors. Professors make every reasonable effort to foster honest academic conduct and to ensure that their evaluations of students reflect each student's true merit. They respect the confidential nature of the relationship between professor and student. They avoid any exploitation, harassment, or discriminatory treatment of students. They acknowledge significant academic or scholarly assistance from them. They protect their academic freedom. (p. 3)

There are a number of interesting observations in this ethical statement about the faculty's role and responsibilities in relationships with students. First and foremost, these ethical norms suggest a compelling faculty interest in respecting students as individuals and avoiding exploiting them for private advantage, meeting personal needs, or both. The compelling interest norm about student learning appears to offer a reasonable approach to addressing the issue of balancing faculty rights with consensual-relationship policies. In the legal context, with any constitutionally guaranteed individual right, a compelling state interest permits certain infringements of those rights. For example, in *Roe v. Wade* (see Keller, 1988), the Supreme Court determined that the right to privacy encompasses the right of a woman to terminate a pregnancy, but the right is not unqualified. That is, some governmental regulations are appropriate, depending on the stage of pregnancy—after the first trimester the state's interest in protecting the health of the mother and potentiality of human life become more compelling than the mother's right to privacy. The compelling interest reasoning also applies to universities—a university has a compelling interest in preserving the integrity of the instructional environment and safeguarding students from duress and exploitation. Thus, with such reasoning, universities formulate policies on sexual harassment, violence, conflict of interest, and consensual relationships that are intrusive into faculty rights.

A second important observation is that faculty conduct is to be viewed in a specialized context—a relationship of an educator and a student within an educational environment, as opposed to an ordinary person in a typical situation. This specialized context provides role definition and some guidelines about role boundaries and faculty duties. According to AAUP ethics, "professors . . . adhere to their proper role as intellectual guides and counselors" through respect, fairness, and neutrality. The duty to respect students enhances the students' autonomy and independence—"free pursuit of learning . . . protect their academic freedom." The duty to be fair to students—"to foster honest academic conduct and to ensure that . . . evaluations . . . reflect . . . merit"—reflects a critical academic value of intellectual honesty as opposed to plagiarism and falsification. The duty of neutrality means that professors must refrain from *meddling* in students' personal lives that are outside the education context and abstain from self-seeking and personal need fulfillment that is beyond the professional satisfaction derived from being part of the educational context ("avoid . . . exploitation, harassment, or discriminatory treatment").

It is our contention that sex with students within the institutional context violates these faculty duties, much like sex with consumers in medical, psychotherapeutic, and legal settings represents boundary and ethical violations leading to negative consequences. As a result, students are often damaged, resulting in a restriction of their freedom to learn. Moreover, through vicarious learning, the learning process also is distorted for many others who are not directly involved sexually with the professor. They do not experience the classroom as a safe and secure place for intellectual learning but a location where individuals have "special" relationships with the professor and where respect, fairness, and neutrality are eroded. These "secondary effects" are most serious and highlight an important facet of our context of understanding. The ban of sex with students has little to do with morality but everything to do with student learning (or effective teaching).

Before moving to the cultural section, a few things need to be said about policy making and the institutional culture of the college and university in which faculty work. As stated earlier, each college or university undoubtedly has a particular mix of variables ensuring a unique institutional culture. In these colleges and universities, where decisions are less centralized and occur in disciplinary-based units or departments in which faculty are central, faculty experience more autonomy, feel a strong kinship to their discipline, place priority on their scholarship, and value interactions with their faculty colleagues. Here, the faculty values of autonomy and collegiality dominate. In these "decentralized and disciplinary units of authority, autonomy, and collegiality," academic harassment policies are perceived to be imposed by a centralized bureaucratic administration that values formal rules over faculty decision making. Thus, the values of faculty autonomy and collegiality become institutionalized as an organizational culture that is inadequately addressed by many consensual relationship policies. These policies tend to be preoccupied with individuals (victims and perpetrators) and inattentive to the social world. Many aspects of the social world germane to the consensual relationship issue will be discussed later, but within the university such policies often fail to understand the cultural dimensions of the topic. In a later chapter, we discuss the role of the faculty and implications of a culturally based approach to education about the issue of consensual relationships. For now, it is simply important to acknowledge that policies need to address not only the interior context of faculty values and beliefs but also the cultural and organizational facets of exterior contexts. An example will facilitate our movement to these more exterior facets.

A male resident in a medical school has teaching responsibility for a female intern. The medical school is located on a campus that has a policy about sexual harassment and consensual relationships. During the teaching rotation, the resident and intern develop an ongoing romantic relationship. The chairperson of the department in which the rotation occurs expresses the opinion that "what happens in private is private as long as it does not interfere with your work." This comment reflects the medical school and hospital culture, so no one brings up the issue.

It is clear that the chair (representing the medical school culture) is at best silent, if not contradictory to the campus policy. This kind of null or negative environment implicitly condones harassment ("so long as it does not interfere with your work"), ignores social issues of the campus environment—power and gender—and reduces a system problem with secondary effects to a personal matter between individuals.

■ Cultural Perspective

Faculty and students resist discussing sexual harassment especially as it pertains to consensual relationships. Male faculty do not want to see themselves as harassers or lumped together with insensitive and "lecherous professors." Women students do not want to experience themselves as victims or lose credibility as a result of criticizing the faculty. For faculty, such resistance leads to a denial of "cultural realities" that distinguish the special teacher-student relationship from the ordinary person-to-person relationship. These realities cluster into two major categories: power and gender.

Power

One element of power is status. Academic institutions are structured hierarchically. Students are at the bottom of the hierarchy, whereas professors are admired for their knowledge and wisdom. Although many claim that faculty power is exaggerated, professors wield a great deal of influence over students, who depend on them for grades, letters of recommendation, and networking. This is especially true for particular subgroups of students who are vulnerable, including economically disadvantaged women of color (DeFour, 1990; Tong, 1984), who are financially vulnerable, often dependent on faculty supervisors or employers for financial aid, and susceptible to negative stereotyping (e.g., "highly sexed," "hot-blooded," "submissive," "loose"). Finally, as Zalk (1990) suggested, perhaps "the professor's greatest power lies in the capacity to enhance or diminish students' self-esteem" (p. 146).

As we discussed, the role of faculty members is often associated with a great deal of autonomy. When professional autonomy is not tempered with collegiality and responsibility, exaggerated faculty autonomy can deteriorate into an arrogant style composed of feelings of entitlement and license to fulfill personal needs (e.g., sexual liaisons with students). The status of the faculty role along with commitments to academic freedom, tenure, and collegiality creates hesitant and reticent students, faculty colleagues, and administrators in the face of wayward professors. For example, there are a number of vested interests in keeping the romantic behavior of wayward professors contained. In bringing attention to the misbehavior, students worry about future career prospects and perceptions of being a trouble maker, faculty colleagues may worry about upcoming tenure decisions and the effect on their close social and faculty relationships, and administrators fear publicity that may bring negative consequences.

Further contributing to the power difference between professors and students is the issue of age. For the most part, although the influx of nontraditional students may alter the mix and dynamics, students are younger and less experienced than their professors. These age differences also carry added opportunities for coercive influence—developmental vulnerabilities and cultural meanings. It is true that students are at a developmental stage in which good teaching can occur: open to new viewpoints and experiences, questioning traditional values and standards, and exploring new identities. Moreover, professors are moving toward a generative stage in which it is common to mentor, to share and teach, and to give back to the community. Unfortunately, the optimal developmental match also can be a time of heightened vulnerability to victimization. For students searching for meaning and identity, professors are most available, attractive, and salient role models. Culturally, professors are often associated with great admiration and, at times, attributions of mythic proportions— brilliance, wisdom, maturity, if not the source of rare treasures, includ-ing "the answer" to the riddle of life itself. Of course, such attributions are tempered in the United States by its historic commitment to de-mocracy, informality, and youth, but other cultures value the aged, resulting in enhanced vulnerability for many Asian students as well as students from countries that associate age with wisdom and authority.

For professors, they may have become jaded in their generative journey and experience the world in dry, gray, and deadening ways. In the throes of midlife crisis, a special student bursts into an older pro-fessor's drab life: young, beautiful, enthusiastic, energetic, and on fire for life. Who could resist the gift, to revisit the fountain of youth? It is in these scenarios that many male faculty complain that they are the victims of youthful seducers. The evidence suggests that it is a common theme in popular culture and male faculty discussions but, in practice, an extremely rare event (Fitzgerald & Weitzman, 1990).

Gender

Sexual harassment is deeply enmeshed in the cultural patterns underlying the relationships of women and men. One pattern is the sex-segregated nature of the U.S. labor force (see Mackinnon, 1979, pp. 9-23), with women concentrated in a few occupations that are low in status, pay, and power relative to men's occupations. In education, the disadvantaged position of women relative to men is well docu-mented. As far back as colonial times, women have been teachers because they cost less than men, and men have been "in charge" of the predominantly female teaching force. Today 72% of all elementary and secondary school teachers are women, but 72% of principals and 95% of all district superintendents are men (Bailey & Campbell, 1992). Men still predominate in the higher-prestige and higher-paid positions at all educational levels of teaching and administration (McCarthy, Kuh, Newell, & Iocona, 1988). This disadvantage for women is well documented in higher education. Women receive less encouragement from educators for future professional pursuits (Gilbert, 1987) and experience several disadvantages in graduate training (Schneider, 1987). On the other hand, males in most cultures are more highly valued and granted greater power and privilege. Although such statements are often dismissed as political correctness rhetoric, a sex-segregated and sex-stratified labor force, including faculty in higher education, is historically and existentially accurate. But acknowledging sex segregation does not reduce the complexity of faculty and student sexual relationships.

The pattern of sex segregation in education often is reinforced by, and itself reinforces, cultural beliefs that men and women differ in significant ways. Traditionally, men expected women to need to love a man and be loved by him, to admire him, and serve him (Horney, 1934). These cultural expectations, shared with several patriarchal societies, were not based on female dependency needs alone but suggest that man's due is based on his feelings of specialness, authority, and sense of entitlement. This specialness aspect may encourage men to feel that what they want should take precedence over the needs of women. Of course, many would argue that such patriarchal views are outdated, but the pervasiveness of sexism in our social world is highly resistant to change because of its pervasiveness in our social institutions. Thus, we consider male entitlement and women's dependency innate, part of the nature of social reality, without due consideration to how tradition (male-dominated tradition) influenced the constructions of what it means to be male and female.

In addition, the cultural associations of women's sexuality and status with dependence on men, and of men's sexuality with dominance and entitlement, can interact in the classroom to sexualize the teacher-student relationship. A few examples will highlight the potential for a sexualized educational environment and raise serious issues of stereotyping, gender bias, and good teaching challenges.

Our first example concerns the familiar seducer scenario. In popular culture, the scene would be described as "Mr. Chips meets Lolita." That is, a scantily clad and sexy undergraduate uses her female wiles to seduce our beloved "Mr. Chips," a dedicated teacher, passionately devoted to the pedagogic relationship, who suddenly realizes that the relationship has become sexualized—"before I knew what was happening." Or as a male faculty member reported (see Fitzgerald,

Weitzman, Gold, & Ormerod, 1988), "It has been my observation that students, and some faculty, have little understanding of the extreme pressure a male professor can feel as the object of sexual interest of attractive women students" (p. 337).

Our description may imply to some that such events never occur, that is, that female students never seduce their male professors. Of course, events like these are theoretically possible and do occur, but our experience is that they are more prevalent in the "mind's eye of the beholder" than an epidemic. Interestingly, in a recent study (Fitzgerald et al., 1988), it was those professors who reported dating or becoming sexually involved with a student or students who were most likely to indicate that they had been sexually harassed by their students.

The next example illustrates how gender differences in sexual harassment may lead to misunderstandings (Riger, 1994). Consider the professor who describes himself as a person who likes to teach others and express his warmth and friendliness to women students through touching, hugging, and "pecks on the cheek"; the student-oriented, graduate assistant instructor, who is young, informal, funny, and spends enormous amounts of time with students; or the instructor who tells jokes, makes remarks of a sexual nature, and engages in seductive behavior. Each of these educators believes he or she is providing the necessary conditions for effective teaching: a devoted teacher expressing loving care for the intellectual growth of his or her students. Whereas women faculty and students are more likely to experience uninvited intimacy, gestures, and sexist jokes as sexual harassment, male faculty (with some exceptions) would be flattered by such sexual overtures. As noted, many male faculty tend to sexualize their experience and interpret sexual behavior differently from women (Gutek, Morasch, & Cohen, 1983). Thus, we hear anecdotal reports of a professor labeling a business lunch with a female student as a "date," interpreting friendliness of a female student as sexual, and misattributing a female student's motives—she is interested in sex with me because of "the way she sat" or the "way she looked at me."

Our final scenario concerns good teaching. This example represents an argument heard by many in the teaching profession: "In short, we learn best from those we are most intimate with" (Booth, 1994, p. 30). As one example, Booth (1994) wrote,

> A male associate professor, John Doe, was accused, at first by one female Ph.D. candidate and later by two others, of requiring them to have sex with him "because I cannot do a really first-class job of supervision unless I know you intimately and you know how much I care for you and your progress. Ordinarily I satisfy myself with the more inferior level of supervision that results when teachers keep their distance, but with a person of your outstanding ability, I think it is important to achieve the best we both can do." Or words to that effect. Only when the women discovered that the same story had been used on all three did they complain to the head about the behavior. (p. 29)

The message of the example at one level is easy to read. The equation appears to be the following: good mentoring + caring = learning. The problem is with the definition of caring. For our Professor Doe, sexual intimacy is the best caring inasmuch as it reduces artificial barriers between student and teacher. Although it is easy to expose Doe's misdeeds, mixed motives (sexual needs), and rationalizations, the example also has several implications for understanding the dilemma of the modern-day teacher in trying to balance personal engagement in student learning. On one hand, we have read earlier about those teachers who have gone too far—the seducers. Unfortunately, teachers also can disengage and harm students by caring too little. In summary, as Booth (1994) so eloquently stated, "the point that must be repeated is that the ban on sex with students has little to do with sexual morality: it has everything to do with effective teaching" (p. 33).

■ Summary

This chapter sought to provide a context of understanding consensual relationships from a faculty perspective. We encountered resistance and related it to faculty values of academic freedom and collegiality and faculty rights and freedoms. Tempering the "rights approach," we sought to highlight faculty responsibilities in preserving the integrity of the educational experience. Resistance also was related to larger cultural issues, including the intersection of faculty powers with gender beliefs of male entitlement and a cultural pattern of sexism. Finally, we learned about the potential for sexualizing the environment when these variables interact in the classroom. Through the use of several examples, we have come to understand that the issue of consensual relationships is more about academic practice than sexual practice, more about faculty responsibility than faculty rights, and about individuals, as well as about organizational and institutional cultures. As the "good teaching example" made clear, the question of faculty going too far is not really about sex but about power and the abuse of power in the instructional setting with vulnerable students.

CHAPTER THREE

The Student Context

It was during my junior year. I had dropped out of school, but after working for several years I decided to return to the university to get my degree. I was in a large chemistry lecture class. When the instructor walked in, he called out my name and asked me to identify myself. I was really surprised and worried. He then said he wanted to know who I was because I had gotten the highest grades on both of his exams, yet he had never met me. This didn't seem strange to me; I didn't know any of my professors. I never thought much about it until this chemistry professor made a point of it. But it reminded me of something that happened during my first semester of college when I was 18 years old.

Back then, I had wanted to add a class after it had already met twice, and I needed the professor's signature. I went to his office and he was very nice. He not only let me into his class, he suggested which classes I should take the following semester. He asked about my background and my major. I told him I was majoring in physics and he seemed impressed. He told me he knew it was going to be hard for me to adjust to university life, since I was from a small farming community and the first in my family to go to college. He was right. I already felt a little overwhelmed although I didn't like him seeing this in me. He told me to drop by his office again soon— he was there to help. I was grateful. It was nice to have a professor who would take time to help me.

A few days later, I dropped by his office. I wanted to see him again and I needed to get some information he had handed out in the first class. We talked for a while and when I was leaving he helped me on with my jacket. This seemed like a gentlemanly thing to do, but then he turned me around, kissed me. I didn't know how to respond. I told him I had to go to my next class and left quickly. After class the next day, he asked me to lunch. I had a class so I couldn't go and besides, I was scared. Everything happened so fast. I wanted him to like me and I wanted to do well at the university, but I didn't want to date him. About a week later, he asked me to have a drink with him. I told him I didn't drink, and I think he understood I didn't want to go out with him. After that, I was really nervous going to class. I was afraid he'd call on me or say something to me, and everyone would know what had happened. One day, he was standing outside the classroom talking to some other male professors and when I walked by they started laughing. I thought they might be laughing at me. I felt ashamed. I feel ashamed thinking about it now, I guess that's why I never told anyone.

Looking back on it now, I realize that that experience during my first semester of college changed the way I thought about professors and the university. It made me realize professors weren't just thinking about me as a student. I guess I should have known that.

I never went to my chemistry professor's office. But sitting in the middle of that lecture hall with 100 other students, I was glad he knew who I was.

It may be difficult for some of us to grasp the vulnerability of being a student. Nonetheless, to understand the perspective of the student we need to consider the feelings students experience when interacting with their professors. These feelings are a result of the interaction of the student with the academic environment and stem from societal and developmental factors. Societal factors include admiration of professors, based on their status in the community and their knowledge and trust, based on the belief that as professionals, professors will not take advantage of the power of their professional position. Societal factors also include the vulnerability of some students, owing to their nondominant status within the culture and the university. Developmental factors include the numerous developmental transitions that students experience while in the university community.

■ Societal Factors

Admiration

As students, we often admire our professors. We value their knowledge and respect their achievements. The admiration we feel for faculty can influence relationships between students and faculty, including sexual relationships. Our admiration of faculty stems from several interrelated factors, but two primary ones are faculty status and faculty knowledge.

As a society, we have elevated professionals, including college and university professors, to positions of power and authority. We give them titles to acknowledge their elevated status and distinguish them from others. Most students use these titles routinely when referring to their professors by addressing them as "doctor" or "professor." Students would seldom call a professor by his or her first name without permission. Students are very aware of the difference between their own status within the university and the status of the faculty.

The role of the professor as an expert in a field reinforces his or her status. The information professors have gained from their experience and insights is important to students, the institution, and the society. Students, their parents, or both are willing to invest a great deal of time, effort, and money to acquire the information professors possess.

Students are influenced by their professors in many ways and in many areas (Pascarella & Terenzini, 1991). The knowledge of the professor extends beyond information regarding a specific field. Professors are seen as knowledgeable and competent in many areas. In fact, often what students learn from their professors is not specific knowledge but the ability to question information and to generate knowledge. Students may change their views regarding a broad range of topics based on the opinion of a professor. Chickering (1993) noted the importance of faculty modeling the way they use their minds as teachers and human beings and the impact of this modeling on students' sense of competence. Pascarella and Terenzini (1991) pointed out,

> It is likely that gains in college on such dimensions as abstract reasoning, critical thinking, reflective judgment, and intellectual and conceptual complexity also make the student more functionally adaptive. That is, other things being equal, this enhanced repertoire of intellectual resources permits the individual to adapt more rapidly and efficiently to changing cognitive and noncognitive environments. Put another way, the individual becomes a better learner. It is in this area, we believe, that the intellectual development coincident with college has its most important and enduring implications for the student's postcollege life. (pp. 558-559)

Thus, because of their knowledge and status, professors have a strong influence on many aspects of student learning. As Pascarella and Terenzini (1991) noted, the effects of a professor's influence on their students extends beyond the specific knowledge of the course material and well beyond the college years. Professors influence not only what students think regarding a wide variety of issues but also how students think.

Trust

"Students often admire their professors, trust them to make decisions, and trust them to protect their (the students') best interest" (Haenicke, 1988, p. 6). What is the basis of the trust students place in their professors? Why would students assume that professors would make decisions to protect their (the students') best interest? Peterson (1992) addressed the trust we have for professionals in our society. She quoted Maslow (1968), who believed that needs for psychological survival, belonging to community, love from others, a sense of self-worth, and self-actualization are at the core of human existence. Peterson (1992) stated, "This assumed agreement is more than a legalistic contract. To place our faith in the unknown requires a level of commitment that raises the relationship to the level of a covenant of professional promise and personal trust" (pp. 12-13).

Thus, a professor's position in this society goes beyond the scope of professional knowledge. It also entails a level of trust that the professor as a professional will act in the best interest of the student and the society. Although placing our trust in professionals enables them to provide the best service to the society, individuals who place their trust in professionals are vulnerable to their decisions and behavior.

Vulnerability Due to Nondominant Status

The university is primarily dominated by highly educated, able-bodied, heterosexual men of European descent. Students who come from backgrounds that are not part of this system are vulnerable within the university system, owing to their nondominant status. Cultural differences, experiences of oppression, or both influence the development of these individuals. Classism, heterosexism, ableism, racism, sexism, and ageism exist in our universities as they do in our society. Potential for discrimination, or harassment owing to these characteristics, places students with nondominant status in particularly vulnerable positions.

Our focus on gender as a basis of discrimination and victimization is not meant to deny the importance of addressing other forms of oppression. Other forms of oppression certainly exist and require exploration. DeFour (1996) examined the interaction of gender and race. DeFour noted how sexual advances can have both racist and sexist components and suggested that women of color may be particularly vulnerable to exploitation.

Gender-related power dynamics also are a significant factor in considering same-gender pairings. Nevertheless, additional factors need to be considered when addressing same-gender relationships. Depending on their experience and sexual identity, students might find the idea of a sexual relationship with a gay faculty member exciting, liberating, anxiety provoking, or confusing. Restricted opportunities for same-gender relationships and the relatively small community may increase a gay student's vulnerability to boundary violations by a gay professor. This is a very complex situation and certainly one that requires additional consideration beyond the scope of this text.

Research suggests that most relationships that occur between faculty and students involve male faculty and female students (Dzeich & Weiner, 1990). Although all faculty-student sexual relationships involve power and boundary violations, dynamics related to gender contribute to vulnerability of women. Males tend to have more power in relationships in our culture and socialization factors support this power differential. The expectations women have, related to gender roles in this culture, combined with the power differential, related to the student role, contribute to feelings of powerlessness for women.

Discrimination and victimization due to gender is conveyed in the following story told by a female graduate student.

I was on my way to a national conference to present a paper on work I had been doing as a research assistant. The man sitting next to me on the plane was a well-respected, nationally known professor in my field. I had never met him, but I recognized his name right away. It was a long flight, so we spent several hours together. He bought me a couple of drinks and talked about his research. He had this paternalistic sort of style, but it had this sexual undercurrent about it that made me really uncomfortable. He asked about my research and talked about how important publications were to getting a good faculty position. He suggested we might do some joint research and smiled and put his hand on my arm. I moved my arm and asked about his wife. I felt like I needed to be careful not to offend him. He was such a powerful person in the field. He told me he had trained one of the faculty members in my department and said he would put in a good word for me with him. He wanted to show his power. I was really offended. I didn't need this guy to help me with my career. I was doing really well on my own. I had a strong publication record and didn't need any good words from him. I was really glad when that flight was over. The next night, he sent flowers to my hotel room and asked if I was free for dinner. I told him I was busy. I kept thinking back over the conversation during the flight to think how I could have handled it better. Several months later, I got a call from the faculty member in my department who this man had trained. The faculty member in my department told me this man was in town and wanted to see me. He asked if they could drop by my office. I was embarrassed and angry. This man was using a faculty member in my department to get to me and I felt that I couldn't say anything. I don't think I handled the situation very well. I avoided them by saying I needed to be in the library all day and hid out at home. The next time I saw the faculty member in my department, he told me how disappointed the man had been to not see me. It was obvious how much he respected this man and wanted to please him. He didn't seem to have any idea what was going on. I remember thinking, the university is such a different place for men.

Hall and Sandler (1984) described the "chilly climate" for women in academia in and out of the classroom. They noted,

> Students attest, and research confirms, that women students are often treated differently than men at all educational levels, including college, graduate and professional school, even when they attend the same institutions, share the same classrooms, work with the same advisors, live in the same residence halls and use the same student services.
>
> Many factors, including familial and social expectations may contribute to the preservation of these differences. However, the institutional "atmosphere," "environment," or "climate" also plays a role in fostering or impeding women students' full personal, academic and professional development. (p. 2)

The National Council for Research on Women's report, "Sexual Harassment: Research and Resources" (Siegel, 1991) emphasized the

importance of understanding the historic and systematic roots of inequality in U.S. society to interact with oppressed individuals in nondiscriminatory ways. Gender socialization of faculty, students, and
other university personnel contribute to the institutional culture.
Faculty-student interactions with women need to be considered
within this context.

■ Developmental Factors

Students also are vulnerable, owing to the developmental transitions they are experiencing as they interact with the university environment. Generally, students change while they are in college. They
not only know more when they graduate but often think, feel, and
behave differently as well. The processes involved in these changes
have been conceptualized by student development theorists. Although theorists differ in the specific factors involved in the developmental process, most see it as a move toward increased differentiation,
integration, and complexity in how students think, what their values
are, and how they behave (Pascarella & Terenzini, 1991). During these
transitions, students are influenced by those around them. As noted,
faculty often are influential in the development of student beliefs and
values, including how students conceptualize problems and develop
solutions. Pascarella and Terenzini (1991) noted,

> A large part of the impact of college is determined by the
> extent and content of one's interactions with the major agents
> of socialization on campus, namely, faculty members and stu-
> dent peers. The influence of interpersonal interactions with
> these groups is manifest in intellectual outcomes as well as in
> changes in attitudes, values, aspirations and a number of
> psychosocial characteristics. (p. 620)

Chickering (1993) noted,

> Relationships which have such potential for student develop-
> ment also creates opportunity for teachers to exploit students
> for their own needs. A clear institutional policy is needed to

counteract suggestive behaviors, unwelcome requests for dates, demands for physical intimacy, or any behavior which injects sexual undertones into the learning environment. (p. 332)

Student development theorists tend to emphasize two primary developmental tasks with which students cope while in college: Identity and moral reasoning or values. We would like to review some of these theories to help clarify the major developmental tasks facing students in the academic environment and the subsequent feelings of vulnerability they experience as they attempt to negotiate these tasks.

Identity

Many developmental theorists view identity formation as the central developmental task faced by college students. According to Josselson (1987), identity is

the stable, consistent, and reliable sense of who one is and what one stands for in the world. It integrates one's meaning to oneself and one's meaning to others; it provides a match between what one regards as central to oneself and how one is viewed by significant others in one's life. (p. 10)

Erickson (1959), one of the earliest developmental theorists, believed that identity is formed through identification with significant others, combined with experience within the environment that helps us determine our own unique identity. Chickering's (1993) psychological theory of student development has had a major influence on the study of college students. Chickering (1993) viewed identity development as the central developmental task of the college student. He viewed establishing identity as the integration of four vectors of development into a sense of who the student is and what capabilities he or she has. These vectors include (a) developing competence, (b) managing emotions, (c) moving through autonomy toward interdependence, and (d) developing mature interpersonal relationships.

A student's sense of his or her capabilities changes as the student takes on new challenges that are a part of the university experience.

Chickering (1993) suggested that identity is related to developing competence in three major areas: (a) intellectual competence, (b) physical competence, and (c) interpersonal competence. A professor can have a significant influence on a student's sense of competence in any or all of these areas and, therefore, a significant impact on the student's identity development. A professor's ability to affect a student's sense of competence and self-esteem is a significant source of power. Zalk, Paludi, and Dederich (1990) noted,

> A professor's greatest power lies in the capacity to enhance or diminish a student's self-esteem. This power can motivate students to master material or convince them to give up. This is not simply a grade, but the feedback and the tone and content of the interaction. Is the student encouraged or put down? Does the faculty member use his/her knowledge to let students know how "stupid" they are or to challenge their thinking? This is REAL power. (p. 111)

Chickering (1993) noted,

> In national surveys, graduate students reported on factors concerning senior-year decisions to attend graduate or professional school. Sixty-five percent in arts and humanities, 62 percent in the biological or physical sciences, and 56 percent in the social sciences said that personal encouragement from faculty was an important or very important factor. (p. 326)

Professors also can have a significant impact on a student's emotional and interpersonal development as well as the development of autonomy and interdependence. This process involves learning to function independently along with recognition that increased autonomy allows one to be interdependent, that is, an ability to balance independent action with the ability to connect with others as equals. Faculty relationships with students can influence a student's sense of autonomy. Katz (1962) pointed out, "The college teacher is a special transference object for his students. He is an 'in between' object, in between parents and the adult relations the student will establish in

and after college" (p. 387). Thus, faculty can facilitate a student's sense
of autonomy and interdependence or foster feelings of dependency.
The development of mature interpersonal relationships involves two
major factors: the ability to choose healthy relationships based on honesty and the ability to make lasting commitments. Chickering (1993)
noted, "Increased capacity for intimacy involves a shift in quality of
relationships with intimates and close friends. The shift is away from
too much dependence or too much dominance and toward an interdependence between equals" (p. 48). Relationships that foster interdependence and mature interpersonal relationships facilitate the development of a strong sense of identity. Sexual relationships between
students and faculty members are not relationships between equals
and, therefore, do not facilitate the development of a clearer sense of
identity for the student.

Developing purpose and integrity are the last two vectors of
Chickering's (1993) student development model. Developing purpose
involves making decisions and commitments based on one's sense of
identity. This ability entails the ability to be intentional, to evaluate
one's own interests and options, to clarify goals, to make plans, and to
persist despite obstacles. Developing purpose involves prioritizing vocational plans and aspirations, personal interests, and interpersonal
and family commitments.

Some developmental theorists have suggested that there may be
a difference in the process of identity development for men and women
(Jordan, Kaplan, Miller, Striver, & Surrey, 1991; Josselson, 1987).
These authors suggest that the developmental process for women involves developing and maintaining connections with others throughout the lifetime, rather than separateness and autonomy. Thus, a
woman's sense of identity is hypothesized to develop and exist within
a relational context. Josselson (1987) noted that identity formation
for women consolidates the personality and connects the individual
to the social world. Josselson believed, "Identity is fundamentally in-
terwoven with others to gain meaning, contrasting ourselves with others heightens our sense of what is uniquely individual" (p. 11). Thus,
women's relationships with others, including their professors, have a
strong influence on their identity development. Josselson's research
suggested that the developmental differences among the four categories

of identity status delineated by Marcia (1967) reflect a continuum of separation-individuation for women. Identity appears to be based on the degree to which separation-individuation has been attempted and accomplished. Relationships with others are considered an essential aspect of identity formation for women. Thus, identification with faculty and subsequent individuation can have significant meaning for a female student's identity development.

Theories of identity development underscore the importance of students' interaction with members of the academic community. Primary to student identity development is the process of identification with significant others and interaction within the environment. These interactions can have a significant impact on feelings of competence and self-confidence, emotional development, autonomy and interdependence, mature relationships, a student's sense of purpose, and integrity. University personnel have a great deal of power in shaping a student's sense of identity. Students are particularly vulnerable to confusion and anxiety during the transitions from one developmental stage to the next. Erickson's (1959) description of the "crises" students experience during developmental transitions emphasized the difficulty of these times of uncertainty. Marcia's (1967) discussion of the various responses students might make as a way to manage the feelings related to these crises underscored this difficulty.

Marcia (1967) addressed the anxiety inherent in movement through the various stages of identity development. Marcia identified four classes of responses that students may make while forming their identity: (a) identity diffusion, (b) identity foreclosure, (c) moratorium, and (d) identity-achievement. *Identity diffusion* results when a student is unsure of who he or she is and is therefore unwilling to make a commitment to an occupation, religion, political orientation, or sex role. This student often is undecided about one or more of these areas, for example a career direction, because he or she hasn't developed a clear sense of purpose or personal values. In contrast, the *foreclosed* student has made commitments in these areas without struggling with examining his or her own values, that is, without differentiating or individuating himself or herself from others. Foreclosed students have not experienced the crisis of a decision. The commitments that have been made are based not on the identity of the student but rather on that of the student's parents, faculty members, or other significant individuals in the student's life. Students with a *moratorium* status have experienced the crisis of a need to make a decision and are actively involved in searching for an identity by considering possible alternatives. Because these students have not made any commitments regarding these decisions, they often feel anxious regarding their future. They are in vulnerable positions, because they don't have a clear idea of what they believe or who they are. Moratorium students often seek out others, including faculty members, to gain support for an identity. Students in the moratorium stage can be particularly vulnerable to boundary violations as they struggle to manage their anxiety during this "existential" crises. Students in the final stage are considered *identity-achieved*. These students have struggled with a crisis and resolved the crisis by making a commitment based on their own beliefs and values.

Minority Identity Development

It is important to note that most developmental theories primarily were based on data from middle-class white men and women and may not apply to other classes or other ethnic groups or races. Some developmental theorists have examined the identity development of specific racial and ethnic groups. One such theory is Cross's (1971) *model of black identity formation.* Cross's model suggested that, although there are some aspects of identity that may be similar across various groups of individuals, a theory that examines some of the specific characteristics of minority identity development also is needed.

Atkinson, Morton, and Sue (1979) felt that the basic tenets of Cross's model could be applied to other oppressed groups. They proposed a *minority identity development model* based on Cross's model of black identity formation. The minority identity developmental model proposed five stages of minority identity development: (a) conformity, (b) dissonance, (c) resistance and immersion, (d) introspection, and (e) synergistic articulation and awareness. How the individual views him or herself, how the individual views others in the same minority group, how the individual views those in other minority groups, and how the individual views those in the majority group is dependent on their stage of development. Atkinson et al.'s minority identity development model suggested that, owing to their status as members of nondominant groups, minority individuals must develop an identity in relation to their own group as well as to the dominant group. Movement from one developmental stage to the next is related to interactions with the environment, including interactions with individuals in dominant and minority groups. Thus, along with other aspects of faculty influence, racial and attitudinal similarities and dissimilarities can play a strong role in student development. Influential faculty can have a major impact on a student's sense of self and racial identity.

The Development of Moral Reasoning and Values

Piaget (1972) conceptualized the development of cognitive structures. His theory provided the underpinnings for several theories of moral reasoning and the development of values. Piaget proposed three basic tenets to cognitive development: (a) structural organization, (b) qualitatively different stages, and (c) interaction with the environment. Piaget conceptualized the individual as an active interpreter of his or her environment and believed that the individual develops cognitive structures to make meaning of his or her experience. Piaget believed that development proceeded through a sequence of qualitatively different stages that reflect changes in cognitive structures. Like other developmental theorists, Piaget believed that developmental change was due to the interaction between the individual and the environment. Thus, the environmental context, including interactions with significant others, including faculty, was viewed as a major determinant of development.

Perry (1970) was interested in intellectual and moral development. Like Piaget, Perry believed that individuals moved from simplistic understanding to a more complex understanding of events. Perry conceptualized three ways individuals might manage the rate of their development to keep their anxiety within a manageable range. First, individuals might temporize, that is, hesitate to take the next step in development. Second, students might choose to escape. Escape is a way the individual avoids commitment and seeks the safety of relativism. The final way students might try to manage the anxiety related to developmental changes is to retreat through return to dualism.

Loevinger's (1976) theory of ego development includes moral, interpersonal, and cognitive development. Loevinger postulated nine stages of ego development. Most traditionally aged students enter college at the *conformist* stage (Pascarella & Terenzini, 1991). In this stage, students want to belong. They have a high need for approval from and acceptance by significant others. They tend to try to belong to a group by adopting the speech, appearance, and beliefs of those they admire. To move from this stage, students need to discover their own identity as separate from the group with which they identify. To make this transition, students enter the stage Loevinger labeled *self-aware*. During this stage, the student moves away from unquestioned belief in the values of the group and toward a development of his or her own set of values and beliefs. This process requires an examination of the individual's own values and identity as separate from the group. As students examine their own beliefs, they gain a better sense of who they are. Reasoning becomes more complex and the capacity for empathy increases. Loevinger called this stage the *conscientious* stage. During this stage, the student has internalized rules and values and takes responsibility for his or her own decisions and behavior.

The last three stages are the individualistic stage, the autonomous stage, and the integrated stage. During the *individualistic* stage, the student learns to value and respect the individual. The student becomes more tolerant of himself or herself as well as others. In addition, the student is more aware of inner conflict and contradiction. During the *autonomous* stage, the student views the world as complex and has an increased tolerance for ambiguity. The student is more tolerant of contradiction and autonomy. During the *integrated* stage, the student no longer feels the inner conflict of the earlier stages. This conflict has been resolved, and the student has developed an integrated sense of identity.

As with identity development, the development of moral reasoning and values may be different for men and women. Gilligan's (1982) different voice theory examined identity and moral development in women. Gilligan was interested in determining whether the theories of Erickson (1959) and Kohlberg (1969), based on data from boys and men, applied as well to women. Kohlberg hypothesized that individuals moved from decisions based on personal consequences of their behavior, to decisions based on laws and conventions of the group, to decisions based on generalized abstract moral principles. Gilligan noticed that women typically scored at lower stages of development when applying Kohlberg's model. She hypothesized that Kohlberg's theory did not fit the developmental process of women. She suggested that women's values and moral reasoning are based more on ideas of care and responsibility of others, whereas men's values and moral reasoning are based on a notion of justice. Support for Gilligan's theory of a different process of moral development for men and women has been mixed (Alcoff, 1988).

Overall, theories that examine the development of moral reasoning and values and those that examine identity development have a great deal in common. Both view the developmental process as a series of stages with periods of uncertainty and confusion between the stages. Both groups of theorists view growth as transitions to increased differentiation from others, integration of new information, and increased complexity of thoughts and beliefs. Both view the developmental process as confusing and anxiety provoking. Perry (1970) suggested ways students attempt to manage the anxiety of transitions during intellectual and ethical development by means similar to those suggested by Marcia (1967) for the management of anxiety during identity development. Thus, the developmental processes involved in establishing a student's sense of identity and moral reasoning place students in vulnerable, anxiety-provoking positions strongly influenced by the context of the university environment, including the interaction with the major agents of socialization, faculty members, and peers.

Older Students

Colleges and universities attract a wide range of students. Although many students tend to fall within the traditional 18- to 25-year-old age range, a growing number of older students are enrolling. The age of the student often is a topic of conversation regarding faculty-student sexual involvement. Some argue that, owing to their age, older students are equal to professors and, therefore, should be considered separately from traditionally aged students. This position ignores the vulnerability of the older student. Most older students in higher education are in either a career or a family transition

(Schlossberg, Lynch, & Chickering, 1989). These transitions can be exciting and challenging; however, they usually also involve feelings of anxiety and vulnerability. Schlossberg et al. (1989) noted, "Adults returning to school are changing their way of seeing themselves. They are altering their roles, routines, and relationships at home, in the community at large, and in the educational setting" (p. 14). These transitions interact with the developmental transitions inherent in the educational process. The developmental tasks identified by Chickering (1993) apply to older students as well as to young adults (Schlossberg et al., 1989). Chickering noted, "Whether leaving home for the first time or returning to college late in life, students will face loneliness, anxiety, frustration, and conflict" (p. 35). Thus, the anxiety related to the developmental tasks inherent in the educational process combined with the anxiety related to career and family transitions can create a particularly vulnerable and stressful situation for the older student.

Older students also frequently lack the support available to many college or university students. They sometimes feel out of place and think they don't have much in common with other students. They often feel different from the younger students and find it difficult to socialize with them. They are much closer in age to their professors. Adult students often are very excited about the new material they are learning at the university but often don't have many people with whom they can discuss this. The vulnerability of older students, owing to the developmental transitions they are experiencing along with the anxiety of being a student, and these feelings of not belonging or not being connected with others in the institution, owing to their age and experience, create a situation in which these students are particularly vulnerable to developing relationships with their professors.

■ Summary

In sum, both traditionally aged as well as older, returning students bring a number of vulnerabilities to the academic learning environment. These vulnerabilities include the admiration students have for their professors, due to their expertise and status and the trust they place in the faculty member, due to their professional role. In addition, students are vulnerable, owing to the developmental transitions they experience during their college years. Students move from identifying with others to form their identity toward differentiating themselves and their values from those of their parents and peers to establishing their own identities and belief systems. In the process, they develop more individualized and complex ways of thinking and interacting. The integration of new information and experiences into a student's identity and values requires a reconceptualization of previous beliefs. Students experience a number of "crises" as they come into contact with new information and experiences that challenge previous knowledge. These developmental transitions are essential to student growth and development but create a period of vulnerability. Finally, students who do not belong to the dominant group in the university system, that of males of European descent, bring the vulnerability of nondominant status. These numerous student vulnerabilities contribute to the complexity of student-faculty sexual involvement. Developmental theorists view the interaction between the student and the environment as essential to the development of identity and values. The recognition of possible differences in identity and moral development for men and women and the importance of considering identity development of nondominant status individuals within a system dominated primarily by men of European descent underscores the importance of creating nondiscriminatory learning environments. Chapter 4 will discuss how these student vulnerabilities interact with the needs of faculty to create a unique environment with potential for intentional or unintentional exploitation.

The Interaction of Faculty and Students

A 24-year-old graduate student came to the university counseling center one day, feeling anxious and overwhelmed. She was having difficulty concentrating and wanted help learning how to manage her stress. At first, she seemed composed and clear about what she needed. She felt that if she could learn to manage her stress more effectively, she could get back to being the kind of student she wanted to be. As the session continued, however, she began to discuss some feelings that indicated a much more serious situation. The student always had been at the top of her class but lately had been having a difficult time getting motivated with her assignments. She was ashamed to say she had been having difficulty getting out of bed in the morning. She had always seen herself as optimistic and self-reliant but now was feeling helpless and hopeless. As the student continued, she noted that she worked as a graduate assistant for a professor, who was also her adviser. She mentioned that she had been romantically involved with him for about a year until about a month ago. The student saw the relationship as consensual and, although she was proud of the relationship, had agreed to keep it secret. The student gradually pulled away from other students because of the secretiveness of the relationship and because she wanted to spend her free time with her professor. During the course of the relationship, the student became increasingly committed to the professor. The professor often confided in her regarding private and departmental problems, and she was proud of her ability to be helpful to him. She felt special. She admired him and was flattered that he was in love with her. About 2 months before the student came to the counseling center, she noticed the professor was pulling away from her. He soon told her he wanted to end the relationship. After the relationship ended, the student was emotionally distraught. She found going to classes and working with the professor extremely difficult. When it became clear to her that the professor was dating another student, working with him became nearly intolerable. The student began to question the professor's initial motivation and wondered if he was sincere when he said he loved her. She began to believe he had never really cared for her as much as he had said. She was embarrassed and ashamed about the relationship and felt she couldn't discuss it with anyone. The student was concerned about her future. She always had been an excellent student but felt that the relationship with her professor might have compromised her professional career. Her professor was highly respected in her field and his recommendation as her adviser and employer was extremely important. She was concerned that if others in the field knew about the relationship, they would discount her abilities and attribute her academic achievements to the relationship. She was also concerned that if she confronted her professor in any way, he could hurt her professionally.

How can we understand what has happened to this student? Conceptualizing faculty-student romantic relationships requires examining the interaction of these individuals within the context of the university environment and the culture in which the university is embedded. Viewing faculty-student relationships within an interactional framework helps us understand the complexities of these relationships. Such an understanding is useful in conceptualizing the dynamics and outcomes related to faculty-student roles and sexual relationships. Moreover, the interactional approach provides a framework for developing interventions.

Before moving to the process and outcomes of consensual relationships, we need to caution readers to be mindful of the distinction between understanding and responsibility. Some critics of those viewing sexual involvement as inappropriate have constructed interactional scenarios in which faculty have been "victimized" by sexy undergraduate "Lolitas." Critics explain that the needs of professors are often overlooked in the rush to judgment by the "sexual harassment police." These critics often point to the relative isolation of faculty, due to personal history (e.g., preoccupied and socially awkward academics) and campus environments (e.g., wrapped up in academic work). This isolation leaves faculty quite vulnerable to the opportunity for personal intimacy with willing and attractive adult females who happen to be undergraduate students. These critics make important points in the context of understanding, but their explanations appear to be constructed to deflect responsibility. Similar to the modern "abuse excuse," models of understanding cannot substitute for accountability. Our efforts are directed at fostering understanding of a complex situation of faculty and student interactions. It is not intended to dilute, deflect, or weaken faculty responsibility but to assist faculty and students in maintaining the appropriate educational environment.

It is important to consider faculty-student interactions within the environmental context. This conceptualization is similar to using a diathesis-stress framework to consider psychological reactions to environmental stress. The diathesis-stress model integrates the concepts of vulnerabilities of the individual with stress of the environmental context. Banks and Kern (1996) described this model:

> Originally referring to a constitutional (biological or genetic) predisposition toward disease, *diathesis* has come to refer more broadly to any characteristic of a person (biological or psycho-

logical) that increases his or her chance of developing a dis-
order. The *stress* (more accurately "stressor") refers to an environmental or life event perceived by the individual as
threatening to his or her physical or psychological well-being
and exceeding his or her capacities to cope. (p. 104)

In the university setting, diathesis would refer to the vulnerabilities of the student (and faculty), and the stressors would refer to the
expectations, requirements, and interactions within the university environment. Combining the responsibility that accompanies the roles
of researcher and teacher, as well as service provider to the community,
with the faculty values of autonomy and collegiality, helps us understand the context of the university from the faculty perspective. Faculty are interested in teaching and learning. They are responsible for
creating and maintaining an environment conducive to this purpose
and, therefore, are interested in maintaining autonomy and self-
governance, which they feel are important to perform these responsibilities.

The admiration and trust students feel for faculty, along with the
developmental transitions the students are negotiating, place students
in positions in which they are vulnerable to boundary crossings and
violations from professors. Women students are particularly vulnerable, owing to their status as nondominant members of the university
community and the potential for harassment related to this status. In
addition to these societal factors and developmental transitions, students also are vulnerable, owing to the importance of the university
to their future.

Conceptualizing student-faculty relationships within the framework of a diathesis-stress model requires understanding the dynamics
(the psychological aspects of interpersonal relationships) of the interactions between faculty and students. Viewed within this framework,
understanding the faculty-student interaction noted above would require understanding the roles of faculty and students within the university context. In addition, because most faculty-student sexual relationships involve male faculty and female students, gender and
gender-related factors need to be considered.

■ Student and Faculty Roles

One of the most difficult and confusing aspects of the university environment is the ambiguity of the student-faculty relationship, due to the multiple roles students and faculty play with one another. Faculty have a teaching role but also an evaluative role. In addition, owing to their position of authority, their status, and their knowledge, faculty also assume a parental role for many students. These multiple roles create confusion regarding appropriate behavior. Relationships between faculty and students are made even more difficult by the frequent formal and informal contact between them and a lack of specific policy addressing that contact.

The autonomy of faculty, in combination with the evaluative role and parent-like position, interacts with student vulnerabilities related to their admiration and trust of faculty, their developmental transitions, and, for women and minorities, their nondominant status. This interaction creates an environment with multiple, ambiguous roles, with a significant power differential between the student and the faculty member. Sometimes, however, faculty deny, ignore, or abuse the power they have.

Teaching Assistants, Research Assistants, and Residence Hall Assistants

When considering the issue of teaching assistants, research assistants, and residence hall assistants, we need to consider the roles they have within the university. Individuals in these positions are both students and university staff. The ambiguity created by these overlapping roles can create increased potential for professional boundary violations. In their role as students, they are not equal to professors and, therefore, are vulnerable to exploitation by professors. As noted above, in their student role, graduate students can be particularly vulnerable, owing to the significant influence a professor can have on their lives. Close working relationships with their professors are essential but provide environments that can kindle romantic relationships. These relationships can be especially costly for the student whose professional career may be at stake. In their teaching or staff roles, these individuals are no longer equal to other students in terms of power and influence and, therefore, are in a position to exploit other students. These dual roles can cause confusion regarding appropriate behavior and increase the possibility of exploitation. In addition, the position of the teaching assistant can be lonely, and competition with other graduate students can increase this isolation. Thus, graduate assistants should be given special attention by the university. University clarification of the role of the graduate assistant and training regarding appropriate professional boundaries is essential. They are especially vulnerable to developing relationships with their students, their professors, or both.

Relationships Between Students and Staff

University environments contain a variety of nonteaching staff. The roles of these staff members vary widely in terms of power and contact with students. Should the restrictions placed on faculty-student relationships include these nonteaching staff? We believe that this decision should be based on considering the needs of the student, the role of the staff member, and the responsibility of the university to provide the best possible educational environment.

Evaluative Power

Faculty have a great deal of power over students' academic and vocational lives, because students trust and admire them and also because of their evaluative role and freedom in determining students' grades in their classes. This power is particularly high in classes in which grading is based on subjective criteria, such as term papers, art projects, or musical performances. In addition to their influence over grades, faculty also have significant power deriving from their influence over recommendations, assistantships, and admission to various programs.

Students can feel powerless in relation to professors. Let us take an illustrative example: A number of graduate students were sitting in a university lounge discussing a topic from class, when one of the students checked his watch and jumped quickly to his feet. He said that he needed to go and take care of a dog. When questioned about having a dog, the student said that the dog wasn't his but belonged to one of his professors. He said he was house-sitting for his professor and taking care of her pets and plants. When a student noted this was a nice thing for him to do for his professor, he replied, "I didn't really want to, but I didn't have any choice. She's my adviser."

Professors have considerable influence over a student's academic success and future career. Students often believe that their success in the academic environment and their careers depend on how they interact with their professors. Thus, the student in the above example felt it was better to take care of the professor's house and pets than to risk upsetting his adviser even in a minor way.

The vulnerability felt by this student and his decision to agree to the professor's request underscores the importance for faculty members and university personnel to recognize the interpersonal power they have in relation to students. Without this recognition, faculty inadvertently might take advantage of the student's more vulnerable position in meeting their own needs (such as having their pets and plants cared for). Likewise, faculty members who recognize their power in relation to their students, and make personal requests of students based on this power, are indulging their professional privilege to meet their own needs at the expense of the student. In fact, they are thereby abusing their students.

Power of the Parental Role

Although universities have moved away from an *in loco parentis* model, the parent-like role of the faculty still is evident in university settings. For example, at a recent east coast medical school retirement dinner, a speaker presented a diagram of the "lineage" of the retiring professor. The diagram was a type of academic family tree, and the speaker discussed the students as "academic offspring" and their professors as "academic fathers or grandfathers." The parental role is most obvious when professors are older and more experienced than their students. But even when professors are the same age or younger than their students, the parental status still exists, owing to their role, their authority, and their knowledge. The parental role can be even more apparent when the professor works with students on a one-to-one basis, such as an adviser. The parental role also can appear in the interaction between professors and undergraduate students. Faculty often are unaware of this parental role and the influence of this role on their interactions with their students.

Gabbard (1989) examined professional relationships in terms of their parent-like role and their potential for boundary violations. Gabbard suggested that there is a growing interest in understanding the dynamics of sexual exploitation by professionals, due to the increase in awareness of the dynamics of incest over the last decade. Gabbard (1989) stated, "Most fundamentally, professional relationships are characterized by the development of a powerful transference element in which a parent-like relationship is unconsciously reestablished. Hence, sexual relationships under such circumstances are always symbolically incestuous" (p. xi). Gabbard suggested that this analogy to incest is appropriate for several reasons. First, incest victims and those who have been exploited by professionals have similar symptoms. These symptoms include shame, guilt associated with the feeling they were responsible for the abuse, isolation and the need to keep the relationship a secret, poor self-esteem, denial, and strong emotional responses (including self-destructive or suicidal thoughts and behavior). Second, responses from those who interact with the victims of both types of abuse are similar. Reactions often include disbelief, discounting the victim or seriousness of the victimization, and embarrassment. Gabbard noted,

> The victims of this form of professional incest have placed their trust in a person whom they assume will place their interests above his or her own by the very nature of the professional relationship. When this trust is betrayed, the impact is often as damaging as familial incest. (p. xi)

The influence of the parental role can be difficult to understand. As Gabbard pointed out, this is often an unconscious process, yet it can have a tremendous influence on our relationships with those in authority positions.

The Indulgence of Professional Privilege

Although professors have far more power than their students, sometimes they don't feel very powerful. Professors have their own concerns and problems that they must manage. They have lives outside the university that they must coordinate with their faculty responsibilities. In addition, professors may feel vulnerable within the university environment, given the formal or informal demands of achieving tenure. Professors also may feel underappreciated because they are paid relatively less than their peers in nonacademic positions. Nonetheless, even though professors may not feel powerful, they are powerful in relation to students.

The needs of the faculty member combined with his or her position of power can result in ambivalence and confusion about their interactions with others. Sometimes faculty struggle with accepting the power and the responsibility they have for maintaining professional relationships with their students. This struggle can result in faculty wanting to ignore or deny that power and the responsibility. Conversely, faculty may not struggle with the power of their position but simply feel entitled to having their desires met. Denying responsibility or expressing feelings of entitlement can lead faculty to use the privilege of their professional position to meet their personal needs. This indulgence of professional privilege results in exploitation and abuse of students.

Individuals place trust in professionals, based on the assumption that their interests will be placed ahead of the professional's interest by the nature of the professional relationship. Abuse of this trust destroys the relationship and damages the individuals involved. Pope (1989) reviewed research that indicates the destructiveness of sexual involvement between a therapist and his or her client. Pope noted that sexual involvement between therapist and client can damage the client in several ways. It is interesting to note the similarity of these responses to the responses of the student discussed at the beginning of this chapter.

The first aspect noted by Pope (1989) is the ambivalence of the client's feelings regarding the therapist, including fear, hate, and the desire to cling to or protect the therapist. Another damaging aspect is the guilt clients feel regarding the relationship. They feel they should have behaved differently and were in control of the behavior of the therapist. Often, the client does not want to betray the therapist, owing to her ambivalence, and may feel empty or isolated. Clients allow themselves to be vulnerable with their therapists. Those who have been exploited by their therapists have an impaired ability to trust. When a relationship between a therapist and a client becomes sexualized, the roles of the two individuals may become reversed. The therapist may confide in the client, placing the client in the therapeutic role. In addition, clients who have been sexually intimate with their therapists often have strong emotional reactions. These reactions may be confusing, contradictory, intense, and unpredictable. Finally, Pope noted that clients often experience suppressed rage, an increased risk of suicide, and cognitive dysfunction following sexual encounters with their therapists.

The depressed student described at the beginning of this chapter expressed similar reactions to her involvement with her professor. The student felt ambivalent about her professor. She respected him, cared about him, and wanted to protect him. She assumed responsibility for the relationship and felt that it had been consensual. She felt guilty about the relationship, ashamed of her behavior, and isolated. She didn't know how people would respond to her and feared their reactions. She felt guilty and didn't know whom she could trust to be supportive. The professor had confided in her, and she felt a need to protect him. She felt isolated, depressed, and was experiencing difficulty dealing with these emotions.

This depressed student illustrates the damage that can be caused by boundary violations created by the indulgence of professional privilege. The professor may have been unaware of the difficulties the student was experiencing, unaware of the problems he had created when deciding to cross a professional boundary. In fact, few, if any, people were aware of the damage caused by this relationship; the student kept it a secret from everyone but the therapist.

Ambiguous Relationships

When students and faculty become intimately involved, they establish dual or multiple roles with one another. That is, the student is in a dual role of student and sexual partner, and the faculty member is in the dual role of professor and sexual partner. Relationships in which individuals are involved in multiple roles with one another often are difficult. Movement back and forth between roles and deciding what is the appropriate role or behavior for a particular situation is especially confusing. Professionals are often aware of the difficulties involved in assuming multiple roles and then decline to assume them. For example, physicians may decide not to treat family members, and lawyers may decide not to represent their best friends.

Dual roles result in complex and ambiguous relationships. The ambiguity in the relationship is due to interpersonal boundaries that have become blurred. For example, a female graduate student was invited to a party given by a faculty member and her spouse at their home. The faculty member considered the student a friend even though she met the student when the student was in one of her classes. The student decided to decline the invitation to the party. Later, during a meeting with the faculty member in the faculty member's office, the student was shown an evaluation that the faculty member had just completed regarding the student's academic performance. The evaluation was very positive with the exception of one section regarding the student's ability to work with others. The student asked why her evaluation was lower in this area, an area that always had been considered a strength for this particular student. The professor replied that she felt the student should be more collegial with the faculty in the department. When the student asked for an example of what she meant, the faculty member said that when she was completing this section of the evaluation she was specifically thinking about how disappointed she was that the student hadn't come to her party.

This example illustrates some of the difficulties inherent in relationships with multiple roles. First, they are confusing. Should the student consider the invitation as coming from a faculty member or from a friend? Does the student have a right to decline a personal invitation without having it affect her academic evaluation? How does the student know what is expected? Should she consider her vulnerability as a student when making this decision?

Multiple roles create blurred boundaries that lead to ambiguous relationships with undefined expectations. Dual relationships may feel comfortable as they develop, but as they continue they may change, leaving the student in a vulnerable situation. Once a relationship boundary between a student and faculty member becomes blurred, the individuals in the relationship as well as those effected by it, need to adjust to the nature of the new relationship. This requires redefining the relationship. This redefinition may occur quickly or it may be a more gradual process. Whether it occurs gradually or quickly, the process of redefinition often is confusing to those in the relationship as well as those who are affected by it. Redefining a relationship also can be stressful, exciting, or both. Faculty need to be cognizant of the difficulties created by multiple role relationships. They also need to be aware of their motives and the position of their students when they decide to redefine a relationship with a student to involve dual roles.

"Special" Relationships

As boundaries are adjusted and the relationship is redefined, the interaction is no longer simply one between a student and a faculty member. The interaction is now within the context of a "special" relationship. Being involved in a special relationship with a powerful person whom one admires can feel wonderful. The depressed student discussed at the beginning of this chapter admired her professor and was flattered by his attention. She felt special. She thought the professor cared about her and she trusted him to act in her best interest. Students often are unaware of their vulnerability with a professor, because the interaction often is perceived to be in the special context of a romantic and trusting relationship. The professor also may feel that a relationship with a student is a special relationship. In fact, the professor might consider it so special that the restraints on faculty-student relationships do not apply. Faculty members may ignore or deny their responsibility to maintain a professional relationship. Being involved with an individual who admires your knowledge and power can be exciting and validating to the professor's sense of self-esteem. The professor feels special, having confused the student's admiration of his role with her admiration of him as a person. These feelings of specialness are true of most faculty-student relationships that have become sexualized. Students often perceive that they were chosen from a large number of students who are available to a professor. They may feel special that they were selected. Professors may also feel special that a young student was attracted to them. In addition, the professor and student often share information about other students and faculty members or inside information regarding the program or the institution to which most students don't have access. This inside information increases feelings of specialness for the student.

As illustrated in the example involving the faculty party and the subsequent academic evaluation, special relationships also can feel uncomfortable. If a student is not interested in such a relationship with her or his professor or is ambivalent about changing the nature of the relationship, these relationships can produce a great deal of stress and anxiety. In that example, the professor was also confused about the nature of the relationship and was hurt when the student didn't come to her party. Students often find it difficult to define and negotiate boundaries with faculty members. They are often unsure of their roles, and their identities frequently are unclear, owing to the developmental transitions they are experiencing. If the university and the professor have not set firm boundaries, this makes these boundary negotiations even more difficult.

Most students would find it difficult to say no to faculty advances, whether they were welcome or not. A student might find flirting with a professor to be exciting and daring but might not want the professor to change the boundaries of the relationship. Nevertheless, a faculty member may not be aware of the nature of a student's flirtatious behavior and may ignore or deny his or her responsibility in a desire to respond to the flirtation in kind.

For some students, the fantasy of a special relationship might be very appealing and may even feel similar to a relationship with a parent or other adult who set inappropriate boundaries. The student also could be ambivalent about the relationship with a professor, finding it partly exciting and romantic and partly uncomfortable and vulnerable. Other students might not be interested in any type of relationship with the faculty member outside of the classroom but feel pressure from the professor. In all of these situations, the student might find it hard to say no to a professor. The student who is approached by a faculty member with the offer of a special relationship is in a very difficult position.

Isolation

Sexual relationships between faculty members and students frequently are kept secret, although the relationship may be apparent to others in the academic community. This secretiveness can lead to isolation from other sources of support and can increase the student's and faculty member's vulnerability. If the relationship is not kept secret, peers may resent or disapprove of the relationship, which can further isolate the couple. If the student has become a confidant of the professor, he or she may have information regarding other students and professors that most students wouldn't possess. Having this information may increase a student's feelings of power but also can result in further isolation. The student feels different from other students but is not equal to faculty. This increases the student's difficulty in defining his or her role. The more the student and faculty member are isolated from other sources of support, the more they rely on the relationship to provide this support. Through this process, the relationship often becomes the center of the couple's life.

The more the student comes to rely on the professor to provide support, the greater the student's vulnerability to the professor. As the student loses power in the relationship, the power of the professor increases. When a relationship begins, the student may feel that it is consensual. She or he may feel a greater sense of personal power as well as power within the institution, owing to her or his alliance with a powerful individual. Nonetheless, as the relationship progresses, the student may increasingly feel vulnerable. At this point, the student may begin to see the trap of the special relationship: To remain in the relationship could result in a further loss of interpersonal power and increased isolation; an attempt to withdraw from the relationship might result in professional difficulties if the professor is angry or feels hurt. If the professor ends the relationship, the student may experience the usual feelings of grief and loss. In addition, the student experiences a redefinition of identity and needs to redefine her or his role and that of the professor. The student now is more aware of an unequal status and may feel less powerful and more vulnerable. Frequently, students accept responsibility for the course of a relationship with a professor and their current situation. This acceptance of responsibility enables the student to feel a greater sense of control but can result in feelings of guilt and shame regarding her or his behavior. An increased awareness of vulnerability or feelings of guilt or shame along with the loss of the relationship can result in increased feelings of anxiety or depression.

The nature of the academic environment also can contribute to feelings of vulnerability and isolation. Most academic environments are structured on a hierarchical model in which status and economic rewards depend on competing with one another. Kaplan, Klein, and Gleason (1991) suggested that environments that stress competitive achievement foster emotional isolation, which increases an individual's vulnerability. Some authors suggest that isolation can be especially difficult for women. Relationship difficulties often are the core of emotional distress for women. Josselson (1987) noted how intimate friendships buffer much of life's stress, including illness, problems in relationships, and difficulties in school. Doherty and Cook (1993) suggested that disconnection from others can result in women feeling depressed, inadequate, guilty, and ashamed. Striver and Miller (1988) noted that these feelings are even stronger when others do not recognize the occurrence of these disconnections. Thus, the isolation and secretiveness of the relationship can make these emotions more devastating.

■ Gender Roles

Most students involved in sexual relationships with their professors are female, and most professors who are involved with their students are male. Therefore, gender-related factors need to be addressed when considering faculty-student sexual involvement. One of the most relevant gender issues to examine when considering faculty-student relationships is the vulnerability of women students, owing to their nondominant status in the university environment and the high potential for sexual harassment. University communities need to consider how gender shapes the sociocultural context in which students and faculty live. That is, how does gender affect the interaction between individuals within the university?

Gender-Related Power Dynamics

An understanding of how power dynamics and gender inequities develop and are sustained in a culture is important in understanding faculty-student relationships. Power dynamics influence how women and men view one another and how they interact. Cook (1993) suggested that analysis of power dynamics related to gender explains how the sexes in some important aspects live in different worlds and why gender dynamics are so "ubiquitous, influential, and resistant to change" (p. 11).

Gilbert and Scher (1987) have considered the dynamics of sexual involvement between psychologists and their clients. They pointed out that, although APA has ethical principles forbidding sexual involvement with clients, there is a resistance within the profession to adhere to these standards. They noted, " Many psychologists refuse to understand the inherent danger in sexual relationships with their clients. They conform with Principle 6a only to the extent that their professional practice is not endangered" (pp. 94-95). Gilbert and Scher (1987) suggested that because most sexual involvement between psychologists and clients is between male psychologists and female clients, the factors that motivate and sustain these relationships reflect a larger social reality involving gender roles.

Gilbert and Scher (1987) focused on the power of unconscious beliefs in determining attitudes and behavior regarding sexual intimacy between psychologists and their clients. They noted that approximately one in 10 male therapists reports erotic contact with his clients, but only one in 50 female therapists reports intimate contact. Regardless of the gender of the therapist, nearly all the clients therapists reported contact with were female.

Similar gender differences exist in faculty-student relationships. That is, most faculty-student sexual involvement is between male faculty members and female students. Thus, gender needs to be considered in these relationships as well. How does gender interact with faculty-student relationships? Gilbert and Scher (1987) noted that research has moved from examining discrimination and devaluation of women to analyzing gender belief systems within the society and individuals within the society. Therapists and professors as well as clients and students grow up in a society that is strongly influenced by our attitudes and beliefs regarding gender roles. These attitudes are conscious and unconscious. Most, if not all, of us are influenced by these attitudes and beliefs whether we want to be or not.

One aspect of unequal treatment of men and women in many societies, including our own, is that men have more power and privilege than women. Gilbert and Scher (1987) noted,

Men grow up with feelings of confidence and specialness granted to them simply because they are born male. This specialness is an essential aspect of male entitlement, which encourages men to feel that what they do or want should take precedence over the needs of women. Most if not all men in our culture struggle with feelings of male specialness, especially their sense of entitlement, when women assert their independence or fail to respond to men's needs. (p. 98)

Male entitlement is ingrained in our culture. For example, the first author recently accompanied her 12-year-old son on a class outing to a local state park to observe birds in their natural habitat. When the class reached the park, the teacher turned the teaching responsibility over to the naturalist who proceeded to point out various birds and show how they could be caught and banded. During this process the naturalist asked several children to help in various ways, such as setting up the net, carrying the bags containing the birds, holding the birds, and releasing the birds, as well as calling on students to answer questions. In every case, even though there were about the same number of boys and girls, when a child was called on or allowed to participate, the naturalist chose a boy. This differential treatment of male and female students was striking. Each time a child was asked to participate he seemed proud to be chosen and became more involved in the entire process. The author's son was chosen to help, and later he whispered, "This is great. I'm glad he picked me." After about 45 minutes, another mother who was unknown to the author, whispered discretely to the naturalist. After this, the behavior of the naturalist changed radically. The next time he asked for help, he chose two girls and subsequently became much more equivalent in his treatment of the children. The change was so sudden and obvious to the first author, she later asked the mother if she had pointed out the differential treatment to the naturalist. She reported that she had. Consider how the male and female children were treated during this school outing. What were they learning about how men and women are treated in the culture? These children apparently were as unaware of the naturalist's behavior as he was but were unconsciously influenced by it nonetheless. They probably didn't view this behavior as a reaction to their gender but rather as a reaction to them personally. How do these types of experiences affect the self-esteem of children? Would the experience of being chosen increase the boys' feeling of specialness and entitlement to special treatment? What would be the effect of not being chosen? Would the experience of a girl not being "chosen" at this time in her life make her more vulnerable to special attention from a professor or other authority later in life? One experience such as this might not make much difference. Nonetheless, this is not an isolated experience for girls and women. The cumulative effects of this type of differential treatment due to gender has a significant impact.

Gilbert and Scher (1987) noted, "Deeply ingrained feelings of male entitlement, particularly with regard to their needs superseding those of women, remain unconscious and highly resistant to change. In essence then, many men resist knowing how sexist they really are" (p. 99). These authors suggest that the central issue of sexual involvement between male therapists and female clients is not love but male entitlement and male prerogative. We believe that this also is the case with many male faculty and female students.

The publications of the "Project on the Status and Education of Women" (Hall & Sandler, 1982, 1984) discussed the effects of gender within the academic environment. Hall and Sandler (1982) noted that college and university campuses provide a "chilly climate" within and outside the classroom. Thus, campuses are not a comfortable environment for many women, simply because they are women. The additional discomfort introduced by professional boundary crossings and violations creates an even more hostile environment.

Kenig and Ryan (1986) found significant gender differences in faculty perceptions of sexual involvement between faculty and students. They found that female faculty were more likely than male faculty to disapprove of romantic involvement between faculty and students. Fitzgerald et al. (1988) found significant differences between how male and female faculty view faculty-student sexual involvement. They found that male faculty members tend to discount or deny the power differential between themselves and students. Even though male faculty members reported frequent initiation of personal relationships with female students, they did not typically consider their behavior as inappropriate. Male faculty members tend to place the responsibility for relationships on the individuals involved, whereas women tend to believe that, because the power and authority of the professor derives from the hierarchical nature of the university, the university community should assume responsibility for preventing the abuse of this power. Paludi (1990) reported that male faculty tend to view relationships between faculty and students as a personal issue, whereas female faculty tend to view these relationships as an organizational issue.

Research also has found significant differences between male and female students' perceptions of faculty behavior. Paludi (1990) reported the results of a study of undergraduate students that found that female students were more likely than male students to label a faculty member's harassment of a woman student as an abuse of the power of his position as a professor.

In 1994, Grand Valley State University (Grand Valley State University, 1994) conducted a university-wide assessment of male and female perceptions regarding the climate of the university community for women. This investigation revealed an interesting gender difference in student perceptions of faculty-student sexual involvement. A total of 12,099 students responded to the survey. The survey included 108 questions regarding a number of aspects of university life, including several questions about sexual harassment. One of the most interesting findings was that there were very few gender differences in student responses to any of the questions. In fact, only one question indicated significant gender differences. This question was, "Sex between faculty/staff and students is okay if the relationship is consensual." Whereas 44% of the male students responded "strongly agree" with this statement, only 26% of the female students indicated this response. Conversely, whereas 28% of male students indicated "strongly disagree," 46% of the female students indicated this response. The remaining 28% of both groups indicated a neutral response.

Thus, there are a number of gender-related differences that contribute to the controversy surrounding faculty-student sexual involvement. These differences contribute to the complex dynamics of faculty-student relationships. These gender differences also can lead to conflicts in understanding the issues and how they can be addressed.

■ Summary

In sum, understanding the issues related to sexual involvement between faculty members and students requires examining these relationships within the context of the academic environment as well as the larger society. This analysis allows us to understand the dynamics of the interactions between faculty and students (the psychological aspects of interpersonal relationships) and develop appropriate interventions. The dynamics of sexual involvement between faculty and students require understanding the power of the faculty role and the vulnerabilities of students within the context of the university. The power of the faculty member derives from his evaluative and parental roles with the student as well as the power related to being male in our culture. Student vulnerability to faculty influence is based on admiration and trust of the faculty member and the developmental transitions with which students are coping. The interaction of these factors of power and vulnerability creates a potential for intentional or unintentional indulgence of professional privilege and exploitation.

Multiple roles within the student-faculty relationship can be one of the most confusing and difficult aspects of the university environment. Multiple roles create ambiguous relationships with undefined expectations. The ambiguity in the relationship is due to interpersonal boundaries that have become blurred, resulting in a "special relationship," often leading to exploitation of the student through an indulgence of professional privilege.

Boundary violations related to professional roles and inappropriate behavior related to gender can be especially damaging. Sexual involvement between professors and students reflect a larger social reality involving gender roles. Men and women are treated differently in our society and our universities. One aspect of this unequal treatment is that men have a greater sense of entitlement and more power. This power and sense of entitlement among male faculty members combined with the power of their professional role places female students in very vulnerable roles. Sexual involvement with a faculty member can result in even greater vulnerability. Chapter 5 will discuss ways in which universities can create and maintain academic environments that reduce the vulnerability of female students and provide an optimal learning environment.

CHAPTER FIVE

Issues and
Interventions

She was crying softly as she spoke, and I found myself leaning forward to catch all her words. She described how she had met her husband when she was a student in one of his classes. She was impressed with his knowledge and achievements and felt he was attracted by her youth and energy. He was very well-known in his field but introverted and shy. They would go to conferences together, and she was proud to be with him. Being a part of the elite circle of professionals with whom he would interact was exciting. At least that was how it used to be. She noted that now she seemed to be depressed a great deal. He wants her to feel better but doesn't know what to do to help. It's frustrating for both of them. He spends each evening in his study writing and goes to conferences alone. She said she doesn't blame him for that. "I'm not much fun to be with and someone needs to take care of the children." She noted that he was doing well professionally, but she was struggling to finish her dissertation. She seemed embarrassed when she acknowledged with some resentment that his career comes before hers or his involvement with the family. She said, "He's very career-focused. It's the most important thing in his life and he is clearly disappointed in me for not being the wife and professional that he can be proud of. I think he still sees me as his student and I often feel like I married my father. I used to be special to him—one of his best students. I could tell he was proud of me. He often told people how much potential I had and how lucky the department was that I had chosen them over my other options. He says that I used to know who I was and what I thought. I was fun and exciting to be with. That's true, I did used to feel a lot more confident about who I was and what I wanted. I don't really know what happened. Somehow, I lost all that."

There is a degree of irony in the fact that academic institutions have not responded well to an aspect of academic life that can cause devastating damage. This potential damage certainly has been given concrete form in numerous lawsuits against colleges and universities, resulting in negative public perceptions of higher education. Damage is not limited to student victims who often leave school, seek treatment, and/or suffer personal or professional damage. It also affects faculty perpetrators who are often fired from their jobs, derailed from their careers, and distanced from their families. The damaging effects often are extended to students and faculty in general. Students, including future teachers, can become disillusioned, depressed, angry, and suspicious of their faculty. A boundary transgression by a colleague can stimulate wide generalizations about the trustworthiness of faculty and raise doubts within all faculty members about their own teaching practices.

For many years, when transgressions occurred, the academy followed the *Legend of the Three Wise Monkeys:* "see no evil, hear no evil, and speak no evil." That is, every effort was made to avoid publicity ("do not air dirty laundry"), ignore the needs of victims (e.g., "be an adult . . . things happen") and perpetrators (e.g., "I didn't know"), and deny responsibility (e.g., "the so-called transgression is a private affair between consenting adults"). Furthermore, faculty and administrative colleagues have been reluctant to confront one of their own for many reasons: beyond the fear of lawsuits and other "whistle-blower" after-effects, faculty are concerned about long-standing friendships, and future professional and career aspirations. As one colleague put it,

"These are not easy things to do. It is often more prudent to mind one's own business."

■ What Academic Institutions Can Do

Academic institutions can do more than hope the damage from faculty-student sexual relationships fades away with time. In fact, several colleges and universities have implemented a variety of strategies and initiatives for dealing with sexual harassment in general (e.g., Rhodes, 1990; Simon & Forrest, 1983). Most of these efforts have focused on support services, education, and enforcement or disciplinary matters. Support services often provide direct assistance to individuals who have been victimized and educational opportunities to those individuals indirectly affected, to limit the pain of a transgression. Education is a natural method of prevention. It targets the problem of sexual intimacy between faculty and students, to reduce its prevalence. Education can take place through the development of clear and concise policies with widely known and accepted definitions and procedures, disseminated through brochures, workshops, and by introducing the topic in existing curricula. Enforcement needs reasonable complaint procedures combined with a positive human relations climate on campus—civility, sensitivity, and caring. What has been missing is a comprehensive framework for understanding a ban on sex with students that is meaningfully related to the academy and provides direction, substance, and context to our remedial, educational, and disciplinary efforts.

■ Framework

In the past, much of the discussion about faculty and student sexual relationships was framed in terms of sexual morality, leading to conversations about how sexual mores on campus had changed, the many successful marriages involving faculty and former students, and deciding "how far" to go with intimacy with students. Sexual-practice-framed discussions often lead to acrimonious debates and nonproductive efforts, resulting in such frustrating conclusions as "you cannot legislate morality."

A more recent framework for understanding consensual relationship issues has to do with gender-related dynamics of the larger society. The question of "too far" is not about sex but about power, the abuse of power, and of male entitlement (see Dzeich & Weiner, 1984). Both frameworks, sex and gender inspired, although providing useful insights, do not promote or enhance educational encounters. More often than not, educational interventions based on these frameworks are too easily dismissed as judgmental, resulting in resistance and anger. Whatever the truth value of these frameworks, their usefulness is often diminished and masked by the personal, emotional reactions of the target groups. For many male faculty, these educational frameworks are scripted to cast male faculty members as the enemy, guilty of sexual immorality either as active predators or as passive supporters. Assigning guilt by association of being a male faculty member is not always an effective way to create constructive dialogue. It certainly may be useful in focusing attention on the issues and stimulating reactions about consensual relationships, but on many occasions the attention and reactions remain preoccupied with blaming and defending conversations. These negative preoccupations cannot sustain extended dialogue, and they provide an excuse for nonengagement at the faculty and institutional levels.

Because of these negative outcomes, an intervention framework that reflects the heart of most colleges and universities—a framework concerned with good teaching—is needed. Our understanding of the educational context has been influenced by "frame theory" (e.g., Goffman, 1974) and the psychoanalytic work on treatment boundaries (see Gabbard & Lester, 1996). The term *frame* generally is used to describe and organize experience. More specifically, the educational frame involves a human interactive context that sets the boundaries of the teacher-student relationship; establishes the roles for the participants; defines the structural elements (e.g., time, place, contractual understandings), content (what is actually taught), and process (what transpires between teacher and students); and offers an atmosphere of security and safety for the participants for them to pursue their educational goals. Each of these elements—boundaries, rules, roles, definitions—"frame" certain kinds of interactions, like teaching and learning, and these framed interactions are set apart and distinguished from others.

Employing the intervention framework of good teaching, we suggest interventions regarding student-faculty relationships based on three basic tenets. First, we believe that it is the responsibility of the academic community to provide an environment that is safe for its members and facilitates learning and development without exploitation. Reactive programs are not sufficient for the development of a nonexploitive campus. Programs must be proactive and specifically designed to address student-faculty sexual involvement. We believe sex between students and their professors objectifies students and creates an environment that undermines the security of students on campus. This type of environment is not an appropriate learning environment.

Second, we believe that defining appropriate professional boundaries is essential for optimal teaching and learning. To establish and maintain appropriate professional boundaries, faculty need to have a clear understanding of faculty-student dynamics, including the vulnerability of students. Developing ways to increase our understanding of student and faculty roles, and the interaction of gender and these roles, is an important intervention step. A greater understanding of appropriate professional boundaries is particularly important, owing to recent discussions regarding student development and optimal learning environments (e.g., Pascarella & Terenzini, 1991). These student development authors suggest faculty-student interactions outside the classroom can facilitate student learning, especially for women and minorities. If faculty-student interactions outside the classroom are encouraged, it becomes even more important to define appropriate professional boundaries and understand the interaction of roles and gender.

The third tenet of intervention, based on a framework of good teaching, is that the goal of intervention is the prevention of harm to the student, the faculty member, and the rest of the academic community—rather than punishing or blaming the individuals or the institution involved. This tenet emphasizes the importance of proactive understanding and discussion of the dynamics of student-faculty relationships in making informed decisions regarding appropriate interactions, rather than focus on punishment or the legal aspects involved. This tenet also emphasizes educating the academic institution regarding the difficulties related to faculty-student involvement, rather than simply developing policy.

The educational frame can be a useful conceptualization for educating the academic community through policies, brochures, workshops, and programs. But the difficulty of educating a university, typically a decentralized institution with strong traditions of autonomy, about centralized policy about what one should *not* do, is overwhelming. The difficulty is probably why the level of exchange in sexual misconduct primarily is at the individualistic level, rather than the systems or community level. Too often, institutional responses have been at the individual level, including the management of complaints and, later, therapeutic services for victims. As institutions add to their individually oriented remedial services and disciplinary practice with a focus on prevention, they are confronted with several dilemmas. How can we enforce a prohibition against faculty-student sexual relationships in a decentralized setting? How can we focus on the problem and institute preventive measures within numerous autonomous faculty cultures? In our litigious society, how much responsibility do universities assume in sustaining the integrity of the instructional experience? Whereas sexual harassment law still is evolving, it seems clear that the liability of educational institutions will increasingly depend on what prophylactic, remedial, and enforcement steps have been taken. It is thus foolhardy for an educational institution knowingly to take no steps to foster the educational frame and ensure appropriate professional boundaries. How much preventative work is enough? Do institutions need to provide mandatory educational interventions for faculty and administrators? What is a "reasonable" standard?

No definitive answers are available. The extremes of denial and avoidance on one hand, and the use of mandatory tactics on the other, are not effective or workable. For example, a mandatory requirement for faculty to attend a sexual harassment workshop represents good intentions but a naive understanding of faculty culture (see Chapter 2). Faculty will likely perceive these requirements as paternalistic at best or representing a subtle accusation of misconduct and lack of trust at worst. Finally, most faculty will not go. Those few faculty adhering to the requirement will likely brood in silence, fight aggressively, or applaud the policy (i.e., preaching to the choir) without engaging in thoughtful dialogue. Without such engagement, the policy is seen as an alien imposition without faculty support. In using an educational frame approach, implementation moves from add-on mandatory requirements as reasonable intervention steps to the integration of boundary violation concerns, including sexualization of teacher-student relationships, into the ongoing institutional activities focused on developing the educational frame.

This chapter will summarize the key issues addressed in previous chapters and suggest proactive and remedial interventions based on these key issues. These interventions include education of the university community, a clear consensual-relationship policy, research, and reduction of isolation within the university community.

■ Key Issues for Intervention

The key issues for intervention follow from an understanding of student development, the educational frame approach, and the three basic tenets noted earlier. These recommendations include

❖ Clearly defining the nature and scope of faculty-student relationships

❖ Educating the university community regarding legal and ethical issues

❖ Educating the university community regarding student vulnerabilities

❖ Educating the university community regarding faculty-student dynamics related to roles and gender

❖ Clarifying institutional and individual responsibilities and defining appropriate professional boundaries

❖ Developing a consensual-relationship policy that prohibits faculty-student sexual involvement

❖ Developing a strong research program to investigate issues related to faculty-student sexual involvement

❖ Reducing isolation within the academic community

Defining the Nature and Scope of Faculty-Student Relationships

The first step in developing effective interventions is defining the nature and scope of faculty-student relationships. The institution and faculty must ask two questions: Is there something about faculty-student relationships that make them different from other social relationships? and Does faculty-student sexual involvement affect only the individuals who are sexually involved, or does it affect other members of the academic community?

We have conceptualized faculty-student relationships within an interaction framework similar to the diathesis-stress model, which allows us to examine the impact of the relationship within the context of the university environment. We believe that given this context, there are significant differences (and similarities) between student-faculty relationships and other social relationships. There are two primary reasons why relationships between professors and students should be viewed differently from other social interactions. First, students are vulnerable, owing to the developmental transitions they are experiencing while in the academic environment and the power of faculty members, given their role within the culture and the university. Second, professors' interactions with students should be designed to meet the educational and developmental needs of their students, not the needs of the professor.

Issues related to privacy and association, as well as constitutional and academic freedom, need to be considered within this context. University members need to recognize that faculty-student relationships are not simply between two self-contained individuals but a concern of the entire academic community. Addressing the scope of the relationship will help the university community develop an increased awareness of the potential impact of relationships within the academic community as well as the community at large.

Educating the University Community Regarding Legal and Ethical Issues

Legal and ethical issues have become a major topic of concern in addressing faculty-student relationships. In fact, the precedent set by the U.S. Supreme Court's 1992 ruling under Title IX of the 1972 Federal Education Act in the case of *Franklin v. Gwinnet County Public Schools* (cited in Wishnietsky & Felder, 1994) has defined faculty-student relationships as a legal issue. The university community is legally responsible for preventing and dealing with sexual harassment within their institutions.

The potential for professional boundary violations suggests the need to consider ethical issues related to faculty-student relationships. The academic community needs to develop codes of conduct that define appropriate professional boundaries and boundary violations. Psychologists and physicians have developed these ethical codes as a way to protect their patients and also to allow them to perform their jobs in the most effective way. Clear definitions of professional boundaries provide an optimal environment for learning and teaching.

Educating the University Community Regarding Student Vulnerabilities

Understanding student development is essential to understanding the dynamics of student-faculty relationships. The development of identity and values is an important aspect of the university experience for students. Faculty can have a tremendous influence on this development. In addition, as students negotiate these developmental transitions they will experience vulnerability, owing to the anxiety inherent in this process. Faculty need to be aware of these vulnerabilities and consider them when interacting with students.

Educating the University Community Regarding Faculty-Student Dynamics

An effective intervention approach requires educating the university community on the dynamics of faculty-student relationships. When a sexual relationship involves a faculty member and a student, intervention needs to involve understanding the impact of dual roles on these relationships. In addition, because student-faculty relationships generally involve female students and male faculty members, the dynamics of gender roles and gender belief systems need to be considered. Faculty-student dynamics related to dual roles include societal factors (trust and admiration for faculty members in our culture), psychological factors (faculty influence over students' development of identity and values), the parental role of faculty, and the developmental transitions with which the students are coping. Dynamics also include the power of faculty over students. Faculty-student dynamics related to gender include the centrality of relationships in women's development; gender-related power dynamics; differences in the perceptions and attributions of behavior; and differences in how men, women, and cultural and sexual minorities feel about sexual involvement between faculty and students. Understanding the effects of student vulnerability, isolation, the indulgence of professional privilege, and the potential damage of "special" relationships is essential.

Clarifying Individual and Institutional Responsibilities and Defining Appropriate Professional Boundaries

When a sexual relationship involves a faculty member and a student, intervention needs to address issues related to responsibility. Responsibility lies with power. A discussion of professional responsibility needs to consider the context of the dual relationship, including factors of trust, vulnerability, power, and gender. As noted in Chapter 4, students involved with faculty often feel special. They often are unaware of their vulnerability to sexual harassment, because the exploitation is often perceived to be in the context of a special relationship. Many faculty want to deny the responsibility they have in faculty-student relationships. They contend that the student is a consenting adult and therefore an equal partner (Dzeich & Weiner, 1984). Concomitantly, students want to be treated as responsible adults, often leading to acceptance of an inappropriate amount of responsibility for sexual involvement with a professor and a denial of the difference in power. Students sometimes lack the experience to understand the nature of harassment situations and as a result may feel guilty when the relationship ends. A sexual relationship between a faculty member and a student raises serious questions regarding appropriate boundaries. As noted earlier, boundaries are the rules, beliefs, and feelings that define how we relate to others, separate ourselves from others, and develop a sense of identity (Caruso, 1987). When a relationship between a student and a faculty member becomes sexual, roles and expectations are difficult to define and negotiate. Individuals learning from these models may have difficulty setting appropriate boundaries for themselves, may internalize inappropriate boundaries, or both. Peterson (1992) noted that individuals who have experienced boundary violations in earlier relationships (such as childhood sexual abuse) are particularly vulnerable to subsequent violations. University students often are dealing with defining appropriate boundaries as they struggle with identity development. This struggle with identity development makes students particularly vulnerable to boundary violations.

The university community needs to consider what responsibility they have to their various constituents. Students are entitled to an environment that provides the optimal potential for learning, and establishing and maintaining appropriate professional boundaries is essential for such an environment. As discussed earlier, issues of good teaching and sexual contact between teachers and students have not been linked. An educational frame with an emphasis on professional boundaries between teacher and student provides a useful linkage. For example, how often do the educational literature and experts on effective teaching recommend a sexual relationship between a teacher and student as a good teaching practice? As noted in Chapter 1, an examination of the principles that underlie the educational frame and resulting professional boundaries provides an answer to this question. The AAUP's "Policy on Professional Ethics" for teachers in higher education (see Weeks, 1995) suggests several principles that provide a foundation for educational practice. These principles include abstinence, interpersonal neutrality, and respect for students as individuals.

The educational frame approach to sexual relationships between faculty and students puts the major responsibility on the teacher, because it is generally recognized that the teacher is responsible for construction and maintenance of the educational frame. Moreover, the educational frame is directly related to the academic mission, thereby providing a more appropriate and safe forum for interactions and interventions about consensual relationships. But, as in most things academic, boundary issues are more complex than presented. For instance, departures from accepted educational practices do not always place the student at serious risk. It is better to conceptualize the diversity of boundary transgressions on a continuum ranging from those that pose little if any risk of harm to the student to those that put the student at risk for psychological injury. The latter is known as a serious practice departure, a boundary violation. But the less serious departures become boundary crossings (see Gabbard & Lester, 1996) that may or may not benefit the student. The complexity for teaching faculty is to determine how students benefit from crossing boundaries. For example, the professor who invites a student out for dinner is crossing a professional boundary by offering something special to one student beyond the agreed-on contract for classroom instruction. The question for the educator is, "How does my class benefit from my invitation?" Or, what if the roles were reversed, that is, the student invited the teacher out to dinner? The question then becomes how the student can most benefit from the teacher's response. Is this a teaching moment, through which an instructor or graduate assistant can refuse the invitation and clarify the boundaries of the teacher-student relationship?

From these examples, it can be observed how useful the educational frame and professional boundaries conceptualization for educational interventions can be. Minor boundary transgressions (e.g., going out for coffee, giving and receiving gifts, nonerotic physical contacts, self-disclosure) can be grist for the educational mill and help focus discussion on the complexity of faculty-student relationships. Such discussion can help shape the position and flexibility of the guardrails (boundary crossings) of classroom instruction and preserve the unyielding guardrails for boundary violations, such as sexual contact, to sustain the security of students and preserve the integrity of the educational experience.

■ Education of the University Community

We believe that successful intervention needs to take place at the university level and that the university administration and faculty need to accept responsibility for this process. Education is important for all members of the university community but is essential for new faculty and teaching assistants. We suggest an extended orientation seminar for new faculty, with a focus on effective teaching that would include a section on interactions with students. This section of the seminar would emphasize the impact of the faculty-student relationship and remind professors and teaching assistants of the power of their position. The section would discuss the importance of faculty-student interactions and the effect of these interactions on the student's educational experience. Teaching assistants would require special attention during this section of the seminar, owing to the dual roles of student and teacher inherent in their positions. As noted earlier, these dual roles can create confusion regarding appropriate behavior and increase these students' vulnerability to becoming involved with their students or professors. A seminar about effective teaching, with a section addressing student-faculty interactions based on the key issues addressed earlier, could have a significant impact on faculty-student relationships.

The university also should offer educational opportunities to other members of the academic community. For example, orientation for new students and administrators could include interactive seminars or panel discussions on the nature of the educational frame operative at a particular university. These seminars would include discussions of the previously discussed educational practice principles, rules, roles, and other basic components of sound educational practice, followed by a panel focused on the dilemmas of boundary crossings and how different members of the academic community (or disciplinary cultures) have negotiated their resolution.

■ Consensual Relationship Policy

A university would find it difficult to defend the lack of a policy regarding sexual harassment. Sexual harassment is unacceptable and illegal from any conceivable policy standpoint (Hustoles, 1990). Nonetheless, policies that specifically address consensual sexual relationships between faculty and students do not have such widespread acceptance. Although the number of institutions with consensual-relationship policies is changing, a survey by Little and Thompson (1989) indicated that only about 17% of colleges and universities had consensual-relationship policies or faculty ethics codes that specifically addressed faculty-student sexual involvement.

To meet the educational mission of the university to provide the best educational environment, universities need to develop clear policies that address all faculty-student sexual involvement. Some universities have developed policies that attempt to discourage consensual sexual relationships between faculty and students. Stanford University's (1996) sexual harassment policy states,

> There are special risks in any sexual or romantic relationship between individuals in inherently unequal positions (such as teacher and student, supervisor and employee, or student resident and the individual who supervises the day-to-day student living environment). Parties in such a relationship assume those risks. Such relationships may undermine the real or perceived integrity of the supervision and evaluation provided and the trust inherent particularly in the student-faculty relationship. They may, moreover, be less consensual than the individual whose position confers power believes. The relationship is likely to be perceived in different ways by each of the parties to it, especially in retrospect. Moreover, such relationships may harm or injure others in the academic or work environment. Relationships in which one party is in a position to review the work or influence the career of the other may provide grounds for complaint when that relationship gives undue access or advantage, restricts opportunities, or creates a hostile environment for others. Furthermore, circumstances may change, and conduct that was previously welcome may become unwelcome. Even when both parties have consented at the outset to a romantic involvement, this past consent does not remove grounds for a charge based upon subsequent conduct. (p. 15)

The State University of New York at Albany (1997) also includes a statement discouraging consensual sexual involvement between faculty and student as a part of the policy on sexual harassment. This policy states,

> Relationships of an amorous nature that might be appropriate in other circumstances may be problematic and may be un-

ethical when they occur between a faculty member and a student for whom a professional responsibility exists. Such relationships may undermine the trust on which the educational process depends. Relationships of an amorous nature between faculty and students, even when they occur outside the instructional context, also may be problematic and may be unethical when there is the possibility that the faculty member unexpectedly may be placed in a position of professional responsibility for the student. (p. 2)

The University of Michigan (1993) has incorporated a strong statement of discouragement into their sexual harassment policy. This statement notes,

Romantic and sexual relationships between supervisor and employee or between faculty or other staff and student are not expressly prohibited by University policy. However, even when both parties have consented to the development of such relationship, they can raise serious concerns about the validity of the consent, conflicts of interest, and unfair treatment of others. Similar concerns can be raised by consensual relationships between senior and junior faculty members.

In 1986, the University's Senate Assembly adopted a statement of principle concerning relationships between faculty (including teaching assistants) and students. The University concurs with the Assembly's position that sexual relationships, even mutually consenting ones, are a basic violation of professional ethics and responsibility when the faculty member has any professional responsibility for the student's academic performance or professional future.

The University of Michigan's (1993) policy goes on to state that the nepotism policy requires individuals to disclose the consensual relationship to the appropriate administrative supervisor so that arrangements can be made for objective evaluation. The policy also notes the difficulties that could arise with relationships between students and faculty that occur outside the instructional context. Finally, the policy states,

In the event of a charge of sexual harassment, the University will, in general, be unsympathetic to a defense based upon consent when the facts establish that a professional faculty-student, staff-student, or supervisor-employee power differential existed within the relationship. (pp. 2-3)

It is interesting that these university administrators and their faculty would recognize behaviors as "a basic violation of professional ethics and responsibilities" (p. 3) and yet not specifically prohibit them.

Harvard's *Responsibilities of Instructors Handbook* (Harvard University, 1990) contains the following statement regarding sexual harassment:

In a series of discussions over past years, the Faculty Council has arrived at a general understanding of some complex issues regarding sexual relationships between students and Faculty members, between staff and Faculty, and between Faculty members and has considered how questions of sex and gender may affect the teaching environment. The Faculty Council has also developed a working definition of sexual harassment and procedures for responding to complaints of sexual harassment. This and other information has been documented in policy statements available from the Office of Academic Affairs, University Hall.

The Council generally agreed that in addition to harassing behavior as defined below, "certain kinds of relationships are wrong whenever they take place within an instructional context." For example, "Amorous relationships that might be appropriate in other circumstances are always wrong when they occur between any teacher or officer of the University and any student for whom he or she has a (direct) professional responsibility." (pp. 24-25)

This statement does not describe specific penalties for violation of this rule, but penalties at Harvard, under the sexual harassment policy, range from reprimand to dismissal (De Chira, 1988).

Universities need to develop clear consensual-relationship policies that prohibit faculty-student sexual involvement. These policies need to clearly outline the consequences for engaging in a sexual relationship with a student. In addition, because sexual relationships between faculty and students are not personal and private, but rather a concern of the university, anyone should be able to file a complaint. The consensual-relationship policy developed at the University of Iowa in 1986 provides an excellent example of the type of policy that is needed. The University of Iowa's policy on sexual harassment and consensual relationships states,

1. The University's educational mission is promoted by professionalism in faculty-student relationships. Professionalism is fostered by an atmosphere of mutual trust and respect. Actions of faculty members and students that harm this atmosphere undermine professionalism and hinder fulfillment of the University's educational mission. Trust and respect are diminished when those in positions of authority abuse, or appear to abuse, their power. Those who abuse, or appear to abuse, their power in such a context violate their duty to the University community.

2. Faculty members exercise power over students, whether in giving them praise or criticism, evaluating them, making recommendations for their further studies or their future employment, or conferring any other benefits on them. Amorous relationships between faculty members and students are wrong when the faculty member has professional responsibility for the student. Such situations greatly increase the chances that the faculty member will abuse his or her power and sexually exploit the student. Voluntary consent by the student in such a relationship is suspect, given the fundamentally asymmetric nature of the relationship. Moreover, other students and faculty may be affected by such unprofessional behavior because it places the faculty member in a position to favor or advance one student's interest at the expense of others and implicitly makes obtaining benefits contingent on amorous or sexual favors. Therefore, the University will view it as unethical if faculty members engage in amorous relations with students enrolled in their classes or subject to their

supervision, even when both parties appear to have consented to the relationship.

3. Consensual Relationships in the Instructional Context. No faculty member shall have an amorous relationship (consensual or otherwise) with a student who is enrolled in a course being taught by the faculty member or whose academic work (including work as a teaching assistant) is being supervised by the faculty member.

4. Consensual Relationships Outside the Instructional Context. Amorous relationships between faculty members and students occurring outside the instructional context may lead to difficulties. Particularly when the faculty member and student are in the same academic unit or in units that are academically allied, relationships that the parties view as consensual may appear to others to be exploitative. Further, in such situations (and others that cannot be anticipated), the faculty member may face serious conflicts of interest and should be careful to distance himself or herself from any decisions that may reward or penalize the student involved. A faculty member who fails to withdraw from participation in activities or decisions that may reward or penalize a student with whom the faculty member has or has had an amorous relationship will be deemed to have violated his or her ethical obligation to the student, to other students, to colleagues, and to the University.

5. Filing of Complaint. A complaint alleging violations of paragraph (B) may be filed by any person or the process may be initiated by the Provost. (pp. 2-3)

Yale University approved a consensual relationship policy in 1996. This policy also prohibits faculty-student sexual relationships when faculty have direct supervision. Yale University's (1996) policy states,

> The integrity of the teacher-student relationship is the foundation of the University's educational mission. This relationship vests considerable trust in the teacher, who, in turn, bears authority and accountability as mentor, educator, and evalu-

ator. The unequal institutional power inherent in this relationship heightens the vulnerability of the student and the potential for coercion. The pedagogical relationship between teacher and student must be protected from influences or activities that can interfere with learning consistent with the goals and ideals of the University. Whenever a teacher is responsible for directly supervising a student, a sexual relationship between them is inappropriate. Any such relationship jeopardizes the integrity of the educational process by creating a conflict of interest and may lead to an inhospitable learning environment for other students.

Therefore, no teacher shall have a sexual relationship with a student over whom he or she has direct supervisory responsibilities regardless of whether the relationship is consensual. Teachers must avoid sexual relationships with their students, including those for whom they are likely to have future supervisory responsibility. Conversely, teachers must not directly supervise any student with whom they have a sexual relationship. Violations of or failure to correct violations of these conflicts of interest principles by the teacher will be grounds for disciplinary action. (p. 2)

A consensual sexual relationship between a teacher and a student can be harmful to the student, unfair to other students, and detrimental to the university environment and community. We recommend that universities respond to these problems by developing a clear policy that prohibits faculty-student sexual involvement even when the relationship is perceived as consensual by those involved. Policies that specifically prohibit consensual relationships are necessary to set clear standards for faculty and to address conduct not specifically covered under sexual harassment policies. Policies need to include information regarding disciplinary action and who can file a complaint. This type of policy would provide clear guidelines for faculty and students.

■ Research

University communities need more information regarding faculty-student interactions, including sexual involvement. Active research by university communities would provide important information, draw attention to these issues, and demonstrate university support. University communities need more information about faculty-student interactions, including sexual involvement of same-sex partners and women faculty and male students. It is also important for universities to gather information about the effectiveness of sexual harassment and consensual-relationship policy. This information could be used to modify the policy or education of the university community.

■ Reducing Isolation Within the University Community

As noted in Chapter 4, often students who are or have been involved in a sexual relationship with a professor have limited their support systems. Frequently, the relationship is kept secret and becomes the center of the student's life. This isolation leaves the student vulnerable to a lack of support if the relationship ends. In addition, other students may resent the relationship and hold the student responsible, making relationships with peers difficult to reestablish. Sometimes the student feels ashamed about what has happened and is reluctant to discuss it. Intervention for the student involves reestablishing communication with others and building supportive networks.

Faculty members also can become isolated. Faculty may enter a romantic or sexual relationship initially because they are lonely or vulnerable and may become isolated if the relationship develops or when it ends. Thus, considering issues of isolation and support networks for faculty is important. University-sponsored social functions designed to increase faculty members' interactions with other faculty and university staff could provide a means through which faculty could become more connected. Faculty and staff dining areas are an example of university structures that facilitate faculty interaction and reduce the possibility of isolation and loneliness.

The academic community can become isolated from resources and sources of support if the university is unable or unwilling to address issues openly. This isolation can be damaging to the university and can result in a more vulnerable academic environment. Moving from conceptualizing faculty-student sexual involvement as self-contained, an issue solely for the two individuals involved, to considering the relationships within the context of the university and an educational frame allows the university to approach faculty-student relationships as a system. This approach reduces isolation within the institution and strengthens the academic community.

A strong sense of community may facilitate the educational mission of the university. A report by the Carnegie Foundation for the Advancement of Teaching (1990) emphasized the importance of community development within the university and suggested that education can be accomplished best in an environment in which each member is valued and supported. In their discussion of counseling center functions within the university community, Pace, Stamler, Yarris, and June (1996) suggested that education can be accomplished best in an environment in which each member is valued and supported. They suggested a model for university counseling centers based on the importance of community that may be applicable to the larger university environment. Pace et al. (1996) stressed the importance of collaboration and interdependence within the university. These authors noted that the more complex issues of harassment and discrimination are not the responsibility of individuals or discrete academic units but university-wide concerns that must be addressed as a community. This process requires consultation and discussion within and between departments. For example, university counseling center staff may be in a unique position to learn about the damaging effects of faculty-student involvement, owing to student willingness to discuss personal situations in the confidential setting of the counselor's office. In addition, because of their training, counseling center staff may have a greater understanding of some of the dynamics of faculty-student relationships and greater empathy for the individuals involved. This information and understanding may be less available to professors and other members of the university community.

Collaboration within the university and shared responsibility for development of a healthy educational environment are important components in addressing faculty-student relationships. Collaboration among university members reduces isolation by building community and increases sensitivity and awareness of its members through shared perspectives. In an article addressing the ethics of requiring students to write about their personal lives, Swartzlander, Pace, and Stamler (1993) provided an example of the value of interdepartmental collaboration. Pace and Stamler, two psychologists from the university counseling center, and Swartzlander, a professor in the English department, collaborated on an article that addressed the issue of considering appropriate educational boundaries when assigning personal writing projects. Interestingly, this project grew from a discussion these authors had in the faculty and staff dining area at the university. These authors were able to address the issue of appropriate educational boundaries with greater sensitivity and understanding, due to their shared expertise and unique perspectives. A similar approach could be used to address issues involved in faculty-student sexual involvement.

■ Summary

The integrated intervention we propose takes advantage of an indigenous approach in which all stakeholders are exposed to the educational contract and offered an opportunity to help maintain the necessary boundaries. Of course, these suggestions do not eliminate the need for traditional styles of rehabilitation and enforcement but are consistent with an educational framework. Moreover, following these suggestions does not guarantee that boundary violations will not occur, but it promises to reduce the incidence of them and the harm that can result.

References

Alcoff, L. (1988). Cultural feminism vs. post-Structuralism: The identity crisis in feminist theory. *Signs, 13*(3), 405-436.

American Bar Association. (1996). *Annotated model rules of professional conduct* (3rd ed.). Chicago: Author.

American Medical Association. (1996-97). *Code of medical ethics.* Chicago: Author.

American Psychological Association. (1992). Ethical principles of psychologists and code of conduct. *American Psychologist, 47*(12), 1597-1611.

Atkinson, D. R., Morton, G., & Sue, D. W. (1979). *Counseling American minorities: A cross-cultural perspective.* Dubuque, IA: W. C. Brown.

Austin, A. E. (1990). Faculty cultures, faculty values. In W. Tierney (Ed.), *Assessing academic climates and cultures: New directions for institutional research* (Vol. 68, pp. 61-74). San Francisco: Jossey-Bass.

Bailey, S. M., & Campbell, P. B. (1992). Gender equity: The unexamined basic of school reform. *Stanford Law & Policy Review, 4,* 73-86.

Banks, S. M., & Kern, R. D. (1996). Explaining high rates of depression in chronic pain: A diathesis-stress framework. *Psychological Bulletin, 119*(1), 95-110.

Booth, W. C. (1994, November-December). Beyond knowledge and inquiry to love. *Academe,* 29-36.

Boyer, E. L. (1987). *College: The undergraduate experience in America.* New York: Harper & Row.

Carnegie Foundation for the Advancement of Teaching. (1990). *Campus life: In search of community.* Princeton, NJ: Princeton University Press.

Caruso, B. (1987). *The impact of incest.* Center City, MN: Hazelden.

Chamberlain, M. K. (1988). *Women in academe: Progress and prospects.* New York: Russell Sage Foundation.

Chickering, A. (1993). *Education and identity.* San Francisco: Jossey-Bass.

98

FACULTY-STUDENT SEXUAL INVOLVEMENT

Connolly, W. B., Jr., & Marshall, A. B. (1989). Sexual harassment of university or college students by faculty members. *Journal of College and University Law, 15,* 381-403.

Cook, E. P. (1993). *Women, relationships, and power: Implications for counseling.* Alexandria, VA: American Counseling Association.

Cross, W., Jr. (1971). The Negro-to-black conversion experience: Toward a psychology of black liberation. *Black World, 20,* 13-27.

Deaux, K., & Major, B. (1987). Putting gender in context: An interactive model of gender-related behavior. *Psychological Review, 94,* 369-389.

DeChiara, P. (1988). The need for universities to have rules on consensual relationships between faculty members and students. *Columbia Journal of Law and Social Problems, 21*(2), 137-162.

DeFour, D. C. (1996). The interface of racism and sexism on college campuses. In M. Paludi (Ed.), *Ivory power: Sexual harassment on campus* (pp. 45-52). Albany: State University of New York Press.

Doherty, P. A., & Cook, E. P. (1993). No woman is an island: Women and relationships. In E. P. Cook (Ed.), *Women, relationships, and power: Implications for counseling* (pp. 15-47). Alexandria, VA : American Counseling Association.

Dzeich, B. W. (1993, December 8). The bedeviling issue of sexual harassment. *The Chronicle of Higher Education,* p. A48.

Dzeich, B. W., & Weiner, L. (1984). *The lecherous professor: Sexual harassment on campus.* Boston: Beacon.

Dzeich, B. W., & Weiner, L. (1990). *The lecherous professor: Sexual harassment on campus* (2nd ed.). Boston: Beacon.

Erickson, E. (1959). Identity and the life cycle. *Psychological Issues Monograph, 1*(1), 1-171. New York: International Universities Press.

Fitzgerald, L. F., & Weitzman, L. W. (1990). Men who harass: Speculation and data. In M. Paludi (Ed.), *Ivory power: Sexual harassment on campus* (pp. 125-140). Albany: State University of New York Press.

Fitzgerald, L. F., Weitzman, L. M., Gold, Y., & Ormerod, A. H. (1988). Academic harassment: Sex and denial in scholarly garb. *Psychology of Women Quarterly, 12,* 329-340.

Fitzgerald, L., & Weitzman, L. (1990). Men who harass: Speculation and data. In M. Paludi (Ed.).*Ivory power: Sexual harassment on campus.* Albany: The State University of New York Press.

Gabbard, G. O. (Ed.). (1989). *Sexual exploitation in professional relationships.* Washington, DC: American Psychiatric Press.

Gabbard, G. O., & Lester, E. P. (1996). *Boundaries and boundary violations in psychoanalysis.* New York: Basic Books.

Gilbert, L. A. (1987). Gender issues in psychotherapy. In J. R. McNamara & M. A. Appel (Eds.), *Critical issues, developments, and trends in professional psychology* (Vol. 3, pp. 30-54). New York: Praeger.

Gilbert, L. A., & Scher, M. (1987). The power of an unconscious belief: Male entitlement and sexual intimacy with clients. *Professional Practice of Psychology,* 8(2), 94-108.

Gilligan, C. (1982). *In a different voice: Psychological theory and women's development.* Cambridge, MA: Harvard University Press.

Glasser, R. D., & Thorpe, J. S. (1986). Unethical intimacy: A survey of sexual contact and advances between psychology educators and female graduate students. *American Psychologist, 41*(1), 43-51.

Goffman, E. (1974). *Frame analysis: An essay on the organization of experience.* Cambridge, MA: Harvard University Press.

Grand Valley State University. (1994). *Summary report of the Women's Climate Study Committee.* Unpublished manuscript.

Gutek, B. A., Morasch, B., & Cohen, A. G. (1983). Interpreting social sexual behavior in a work setting. *Journal of Vocational Behavior, 22,* 30-48.

Haenicke, D. H. (1988). Ethics in academia. *Papers presented to the Center for the Study of Ethics in Society, 1*(2), 1-15.

Hall, R. M., & Sandler, B. R. (1982). *The classroom climate: A chilly one for women?* Washington, DC: Project on the Status and Education of Women, Association of American Colleges.

Hall, R. M., & Sandler, B. R. (1984). *Out of the classroom: A chilly campus climate for women?* Washington, DC: Project on the Status and Education of Women, Association of American Colleges.

Harvard University. (1990). *Responsibilities of instructors handbook.* Cambridge, MA: Author.

Hoffman, F. (1986). Sexual harassment in academia: Feminist theory and institutional practice. *Harvard Educational Review, 56,* 105-121.

Horney, K. (1934). The overevaluation of love: A study of a common present-day feminine type. *Psychoanalytic Quarterly, 3,* 605-638.

Hustoles, T. (1990). Consensual relations issues in higher education. In E. K. Cole, (Ed.), *Sexual harassment on campus: A legal compendium* (2nd ed., pp. 1-5). Washington, DC: National Association of College and University Attorneys.

Jordan, J. V., Kaplan, A. G., Miller, J. B., Striver, I. P., & Surrey, J. L. (Eds.). (1991). *Women's growth in connection: Writings from the Stone Center.* New York: Guilford.

Josselson, R. (1987). *Finding herself: Pathways to identity development in women.* San Francisco: Jossey-Bass.

Kaplan, A., Klein, R., & Gleason, N. (1991). Women's self development in late adolescence. In J. V. Jordan, A. G. Kaplan, J. B. Miller, I. P. Stiver, & J. L. Surrey (Eds.), *Women's growth in connection: Writings from the Stone Center* (Work in Progress No. 17, pp. 122-140). New York: Guilford.

Katz, J. (1962). Personality and interpersonal relations in the college classroom. In N. Sanford (Ed.), *The American college.* New York: Wiley.

Keller, E. A. (1988). Consensual amorous relationships between faculty and students: The constitutional right to privacy. *Journal of College and University Law, 15,* 21-42.

Kenig, S., & Ryan, J. (1986). Sex differences in levels of tolerance and attribution of blame for sexual harassment on a university campus. *Sex Roles, 15,* 535-549.

Kohlberg, L. (1969). Stage and sequence: The cognitive-development approach to socialization. In D. Goslin (Ed.), *Handbook of socialization theory and research.* Chicago: Rand McNally.

Korf v. Ball State University, 726 F.2d 122 (7th Cir. 1984).

Kuh, G. D. (Ed.). (1993). *Cultural perspectives in student affairs work.* Lanham, MD: American College Personnel Association.

Little, D., & Thompson, J. (1989). Campus policies, the law, and sexual relationships. *Thought and Action, 5*(1), 17-24.

Loevinger, J. (1976). *Ego development: Conceptions and theories.* San Francisco: Jossey-Bass.

Mackinnon, C. A. (1979). *Sexual harassment of working women: A case of sex discrimination.* New Haven, CT: Yale University Press.

Marcia, J. (1967). Ego identity status: Relationship to change in self-esteem, "general maladjustment," and authoritarianism. *Journal of Personality, 35,* 118 -133.

Maslow, A. (1968). *Toward a psychology of being.* New York: Van Nostrand Reinhold.

McCarthy, M. M., Kuh, G. D., Newell, L. J., & Iocona, C. M. (1988). *Under scrutiny: The educational administration professorate.* Tempe, AZ: University Council of Educational Administrators.

Naragon v. Wharton, 737 F.2d 1402 (5th Cir. 1984).

Pace, D., Stamler, V. L., Yarris, E., & June, L. (1996). Rounding out the cube: Evolution to a global model for counseling centers. *Journal of Counseling and Development, 74,* 321-325.

Paludi, M. A. (1990). Creating new taboos in the academy: Faculty responsibility in preventing sexual harassment. *Initiatives, 52*(4), 29-33.

Pascarella, E. T., & Terenzini, P. T. (1991). *How college affects students.* San Francisco: Jossey-Bass.

Perry, W. (1970). *Forms of intellectual and ethical development in college years: A scheme.* New York: Holt, Rinehart, & Winston.

Peterson, M. R. (1992). *At personal risk: Boundary violations in professional-client relationships.* New York: Norton.

Piaget, J. (1972). Intellectual evolution from adolescence to adulthood. *Human Development, 15,* 1-12.

Pitulla, J. (1992, November). Unfair Advantage. *American Bar Association Journal,* 76-80.

Pope, K. S. (1989). Teacher-student sexual intimacy. In G. O. Gabbard (Ed.), *Sexual exploitation in professional relationships* (pp. 163-176). Washington, DC: American Psychiatric Press.

Renzetti, C. M., & Miley, C. H. (Eds.). (1996). *Violence in gay and lesbian domestic partnerships.* Binghamton, NY: Harrington Park Press.

Rhodes, F. H. T. (1990). The moral imperative to prevent sexual harassment on campus. *Journal of NAWDAC, 52,* 1-4.

Riger, S. (1994). Gender dilemmas in sexual harassment policies and procedures. *American Psychologist, 46,* 497-505.

Rosch, E. (1973). On the internal structure of perceptual and semantic categories. In T. E. Moore (Ed.), *Cognitive development and the acquisition of language* (pp. 112-144). New York: Academic Press.

Rosch, E. (1978). Principles of categorization. In E. Rosch & B. Lloyd (Eds.), *Cognition and categorization*. Hillsdale, NJ: Lawrence Erlbaum.

Rosovsky, H. (1990). *The university: An owner's manual.* New York: Norton.

Rudolph, F. (1962). *The American college and university.* New York: Vintage Books.

Schlosberg, N. K., Lynch, A. Q., & Chickering, A. W. (1989). *Improving higher education environments for adults: Responsive programs and services from entry to departure.* San Francisco: Jossey-Bass.

Schneider, B. E. (1987). Graduate women, sexual harassment, and university policy. *Journal of Higher Education, 58,* 46-65.

Siegel, D. L. (1991). *Sexual harassment: Research and resources (A report in progress).* New York: National Council for Research on Women.

Simon, L. A. K., & Forrest, L. (1983). Implementing a sexual harassment program at a large university. *Journal of NAWDAC, 46,* 55-61.

Sipchen, B. (1994, September 16). A lesson in love? The latest campus debate is whether student-professor romances are about power or passion. *Los Angeles Times,* E1, E6.

Stanford University. (1996). *Sexual harassment policy: Note on consensual relationships (Section 6).* Palo Alto, CA: Author.

State University of New York at Albany. (1997). *Policy on sexual harassment.* Albany: Author.

Stites, M. C. (1996). University consensual relationship policies. In M. Paludi (Ed.), *Sexual harassment on college campuses: Abusing the ivory power* (pp. 153-175). Albany: State University of New York Press.

Striver, I. P., & Miller, J. B. (1988). *From depression to sadness in women's psychotherapy.* (Work in Progress No. 36). Wellesley, MA: Stone Center for Developmental Services and Studies.

Swartzlander, S., Pace, D., & Stamler, V. L., (1993, February 17). The ethics of requiring students to write about their personal lives. *The Chronicle of Higher Education,* pp. B1-B2.

Tong, R. (1984). *Women, sex, and the law.* Totowa, NJ: Rowman and Allanheld.

University of Iowa. (1986). *University policy on sexual harassment and consensual relationships.* Iowa City, IA: Author.

University of Michigan. (1993). *Sexual harassment policy.* Ann Arbor, MI: Author.

Wagner, K. C. (1993, May 26). Fantasies of true love in academe. *The Chronicle of Higher Education,* pp. B1-B3.

Weeks, K. M. (1995, Summer). Consensual sexual relationships and policy development. *Lex Collegii, 19,* 1-6.

White, W. L. (1986). *Incest in the organizational family: The ecology of burnout in closed systems.* Bloomington, IL: Lighthouse Training Institute.

Wishnietsky, D. H., & Felder, D. (1994). The effect of Franklin v. Gwinnett County on sexual harassment policy in secondary education. *Initiatives, 56*(1), 37-41.

Yale University. (1997). *Policies on sexual harassment and sexual relations between teachers and students.* New Haven, CT: Author.

Zalk, S. R. (1990). Men in the academy: A psychological profile of harassment. In M. Paludi (Ed.), *Ivory power: Sexual harassment on campus* (pp. 141-175). Albany: State University of New York Press.

Zalk, S. R., Paludi, M., & Dederich, J. (1990). Women student assessment of consensual relationships with their professors: Ivory power reconsidered. In E. K. Cole (Ed.), *Sexual harassment on campus: A legal compendium* (2nd. ed., pp. 103-132). Washington, DC: National Association of College and University Attorneys.

Index

About the Authors

Virginia Lee Stamler is a licensed psychologist in private practice in Iowa City, Iowa. She received her B.S. degree in psychology from the State University of New York at Binghamton in 1977 and her M.A. (1979) and Ph.D. (1987) from the University of Iowa.

Previously, she served as the Director of Doctoral Internship Training at the Career Planning and Counseling Center at Grand Valley State University, Senior Staff Psychologist at Boston University, and Senior Staff Psychologist at the University of Iowa. Her research interests focus on mental health issues within higher education.

Gerald L. Stone is Director of the University Counseling Service and Professor of Counseling Psychology at the University of Iowa. He received his B.A. degree in Psychology at UCLA (1963) and his M.A. (1970) and Ph.D. (1972) from Michigan State University.

Previously, he served as the Chair of Applied Psychology Programmes and Chair of the Counseling Psychology Programme within the Department of Psychology at the University of Western Ontario. His research interests focus on mental health policy and practice in higher education.